GW01471613

Kindle Fire Essential Guide

Kindle Fire Essential Guide

Comprehensive User Guide with Tips, Tricks & Advanced Tweaks for the Amazon Kindle Fire

Ned Kubica

Acknowledgements

Thank you to the extremely talented Youzell Jeffers at digizell.com for designing the cover artwork for this book.

Thank you to my family and friends for always being so wonderful. You inspire me every single day.

And of course to you for purchasing this book, thank you most of all.

Kindle Fire Essential Guide

Comprehensive User Guide with Tips, Tricks as well as Advanced Tweaks for the Amazon Kindle Fire.

Copyright © 2011 by Ned Kubica

Printed in the United States of America

Legal

All Rights Reserved. No part of this work may be reproduced or transmitted in any forms or means, electronic or mechanical, including photocopying, recording, or by any information storage or retrieval system, without the prior written permission of the copyright owner and publisher.

ISBN-13: 978-0-9849246-1-5
ISBN-10: 0-984-92461-2

Trademarked names, logos, and images may appear in this book. Rather than use a trademark symbol with every occurrence of a trademarked name, logo, or image we use the names, logos, and images only in an editorial fashion and to the benefit of the trademark owner, with no intention of infringement of the trademark.

The use in this publication of trade names, trademarks, service marks, and similar terms, even if they are not identified as such, is not to be taken as an expression of opinion as to whether or not they are subject to proprietary rights.

The information in this book is distributed on an "as is" basis, without warranty. Although every precaution has been taken in the preparation of this work, neither Ned Kubica nor any entity shall have any liability with respect to any loss or damage caused or alleged to be caused directly or indirectly by the information contained in this book.

This is Edition 1.1 of the printed version of this book for record keeping purposes. Any changes to this book will be reflected by an increase of this number.

In an Agreement with Amazon.com the electronic version of this paperback book is available exclusively to readers of the Kindle eBook Store, Amazon.com Lending Library and the eBook Store on all Kindle devices.

Amazon Prime Members may download the electronic version of this book for Free from the Kindle Owners' Lending Library.

Distribution of electronic formats may change in the future.

About the Author

Ned Kubica is a software engineer and web architect who creates and distributes software applications for the iOS (iPad, iPhone and iPod Touch) and Android OS. He is the proud owner of multiple mobile devices including an iPad 2, iPhone 4S and Kindle Fire.

Contents

Introduction to the Kindle Fire

Congratulations and welcome to the Amazon Kindle Fire. You have an amazing device with the capability to surf the Internet, send and receive E-Mail messages, listen to music, watch and stream videos and more.

The following guide was created to help new and existing Kindle and/or Kindle Fire owners learn some of the important yet infrequently discussed features of the device. Feel free to bookmark any pages or jump to a specific area using the Table of Contents if you are looking for something specific.

Sit back, relax and enjoy all that your Amazon Fire has to offer.

The Basics

Powering on and off

There is only one button on the Kindle Fire. Press and Hold down on this button when your device is powered on to access the Shutdown Menu.

Choose either Shut Down or Cancel from this menu.

To Power the device on, tap the button once when off.

To put your device in Sleep Mode press the button once.

Charging the Kindle Fire

When you first get your Kindle or at the very first opportunity plug it in and charge for a complete four hours. This will ensure you experience great battery life with your device.

To charge the Kindle Fire plug-in the included cable into the charging slot on your device. Using a non-stock charger is not recommended.

Controlling the Screen

You control the Kindle Fire with your finger or a compatible stylus. For the best experience using your finger is recommended.

Single-Tap – Tap the screen much like you would a mouse click. Tap on an icon or an area of the screen you wish to interact with.

Double-Tap – Tapping the screen twice in quick succession will display other content where enabled on your device.

Tap and Hold – Place your finger on the screen on an icon or an area and hold down until a menu appears.

Pinch and Pull – When you are viewing content that has this feature enabled you can use your fingers to pinch your fingers together and apart to control the dimensions and orientations of photos, maps and other content.

Swipe – Swiping left to right on the screen will present interactive movements to objects on the screen. You can use the Swipe feature to control the carrousel in the middle of the main screen.

Introduction to the Status Bar

Ned's kindle 3   6:40   ⚙ 🛜 🔋

At the top of the screen you will see notifications. These can come from apps, e-mail messages, and other things like the music player.

Introduction to the Carousel

Much like a log of all recent activity, the Carousel will display recently accessed music, books, web pages and apps for you to interact with.

Swipe with your finger to scroll through the content.

Changing the Device Brightness

Tap the settings icon in the top right corner of your Fire.

Now tap Brightness. Use the slider that appears to adjust the brightness that is comfortable to you.

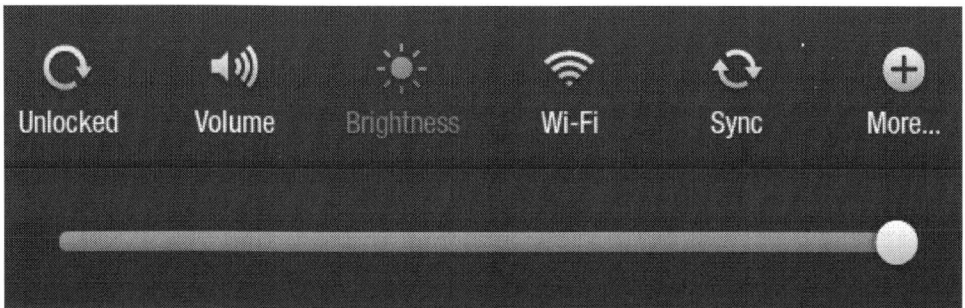

Screen Orientation

The Kindle Fire can be viewed in Portrait or Landscape mode. To prevent switching to another orientation tap the settings icon in the top right corner of your Fire to access your settings.

Tap Unlocked to Lock the orientation.

Repeat the process to Unlock.

Finding things quickly

Search the content, apps, music and more on your device at any time from your home screen by tapping the Search bar at the top of the screen, entering your search query and selecting the appropriate file.

Tap and hold search results to add to your favorites or tap it once to open it.

Accessing your Apps

From the main screen tap Apps.
You will be presented with a list of your Applications.

The Kindle Fire comes pre-loaded with a few apps.

To download more:

Tap Store to Browse for paid and free apps.

Tap Cloud to view the Apps that you have stored in your cloud account or tap Device to view Apps that are stored locally.

Ned's kindle ①   6:23   ⚙ 📶 🔋

Apps   Cloud   Device   Store ›

By Recent   By Title

Pandora   Email   Corona Indi...   Pulse   The Wall Str...

Jewels   Gallery   WIRED Mag...   Contacts   iHeartRadio

amazon

Shop   Angry Birds ...   Twitter Mobi...   The Weathe...   Little Piano (...

Airport Mani...   Facebook   Help & Feed...   Quickoffice, ...   Audible

IMDb

🏠   ⬅   🔍

Ned's kindle 1   6:23   ⚙ 🛜 🔋

Apps

Cloud   **Device**   Store >

By Recent   By Title

Pandora   Email   Corona Indi…   Pulse   The Wall Str…

Jewels   Jewels   Gallery   WIRED Mag…   Contacts

iHeartRadio   Shop   Angry Birds …   Twitter Mobi…   The Weathe…

Little Piano (…   Airport Mani…   Facebook   Help & Feed…   Quickoffice, …

Comics   ESPN Score…   Words With …   Audible   IMDb

🏠   ←   🔍

Starting an App

From the main screen tap Apps.
From the list of your Apps tap the Application Icon to begin.

Adding an App to your Favorites

In the middle on the main screen you see a carrousel of items. To add one of these Applications to your Favorites, tap and hold down on the icon until you see "Add to Favorites". Tap it to complete the process.

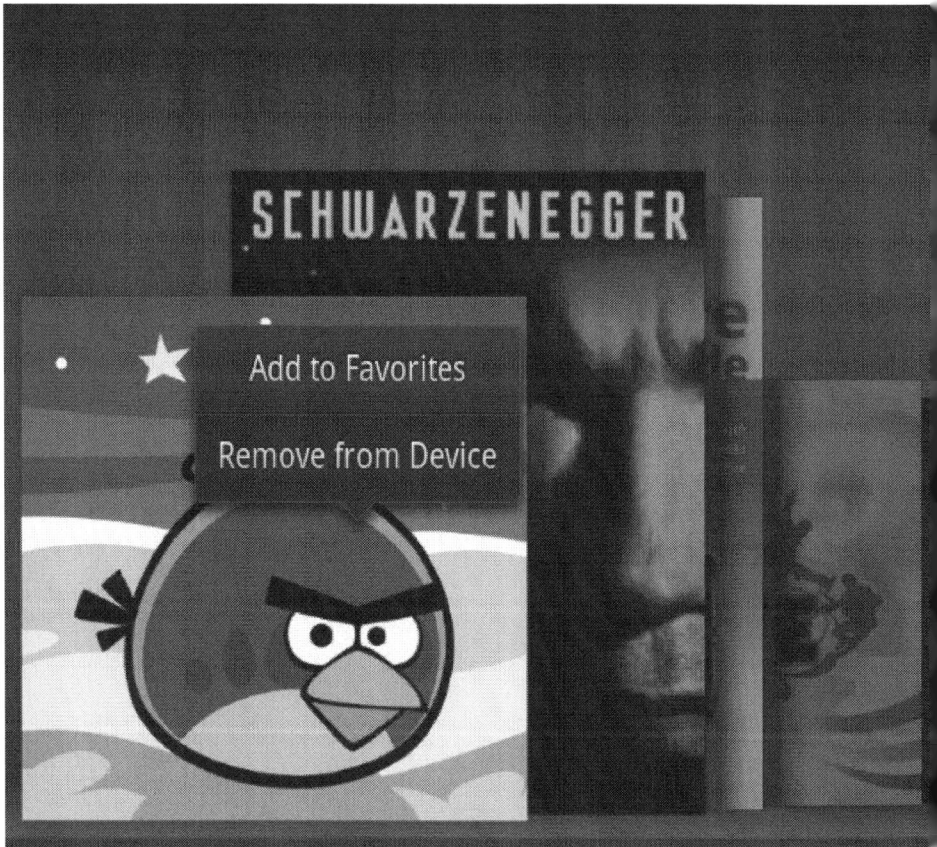

Removing Apps from your Favorites

To remove an Application from your favorites tap and hold down on the icon until "Remove from Favorites" appears. Tap it to complete.

Checking Battery Strength & Storage Space

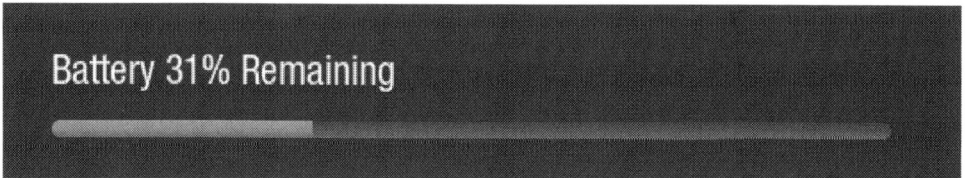

Battery 31% Remaining

From the top right-hand corner of your screen tap the settings icon.

Tap More. Tap Device.

Your current device usage and battery levels will be shown.

Reading a Book

From the main screen tap Books.

Select the cover of the book or file you wish to read.
Use your finger to swipe left to right to control the page.
Tap the screen once to display the menu and again to hide.
Tap the Home icon that appears to return to the main screen.
To increase the size of the font used in the material tap Aa.
To bookmark a page tap the ribbon icon in the top right corner.

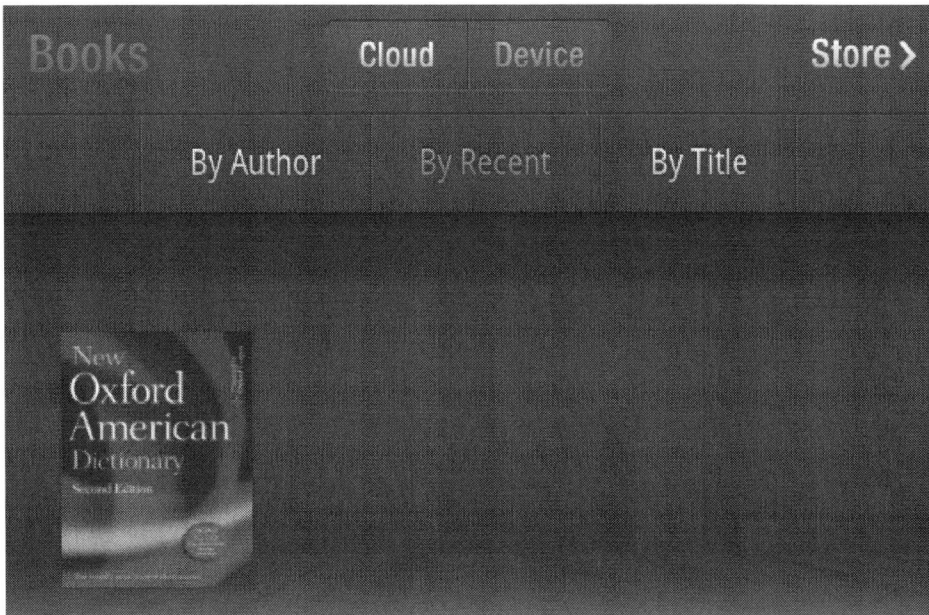

Tap Cloud at the top of your screen to view the books that are stored in your account but are not yet on your device.

To download one of the Books in the Cloud to your Device tap the down arrow you see shown below.

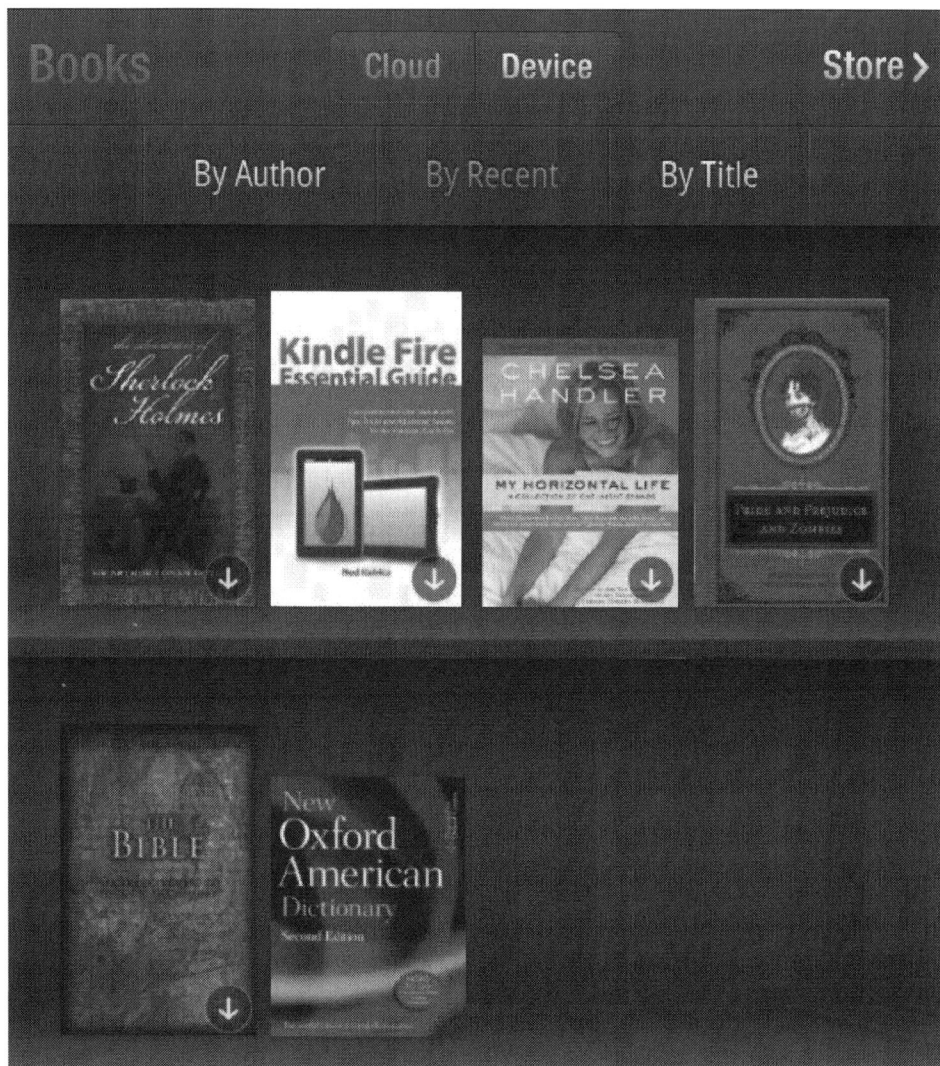

Documents & Files

From the main screen tap Documents.

You will be presented with a personalized email address to send documents and files to your device. You have the option of changing this address online at www.amazon.com.

You will receive an e-mail message when the document is available on your device. Documents must be sent from approved addresses only. View and change approved senders online at www.amazon.com

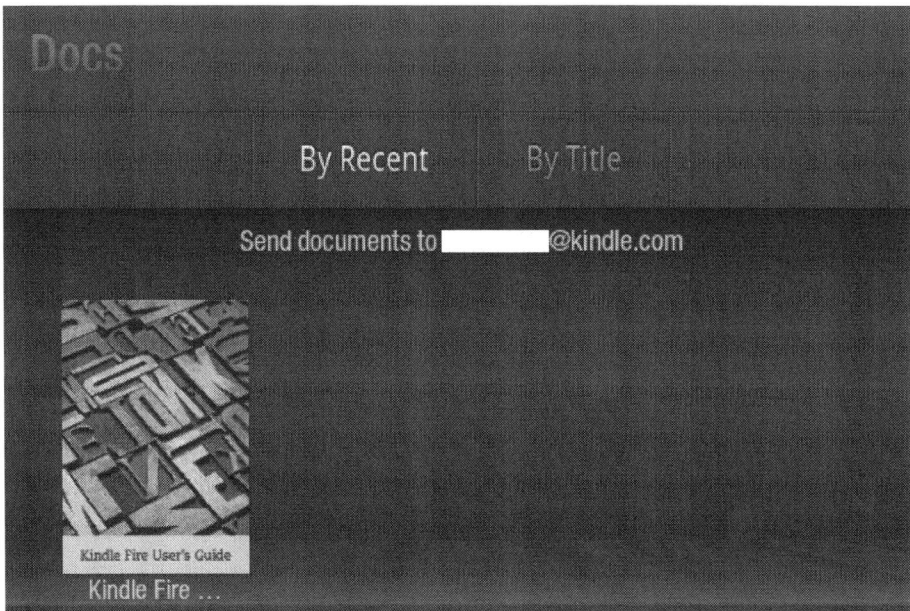

Watch a Video

From the main screen tap Video.
Select the title you wish to view with your finger to start playback. Tap Library to view content you already own or have access to.

Tap Store to return to the Store to purchase or stream content.

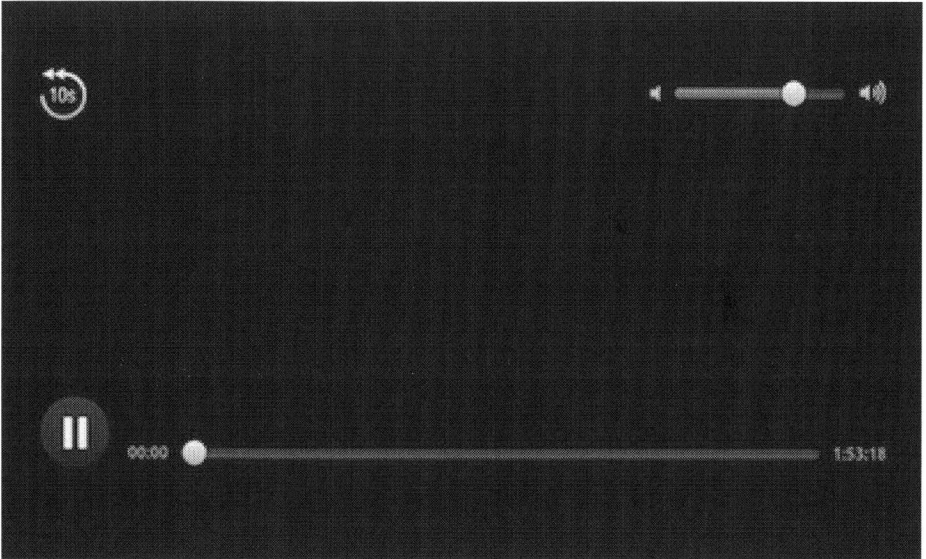

Watch an Amazon Prime Video

From the main screen tap Video.

Select Prime Instant Videos.
Select the cover of the content you want to view.

Tap Watch Now to begin playback.
Rotate your device if necessary.

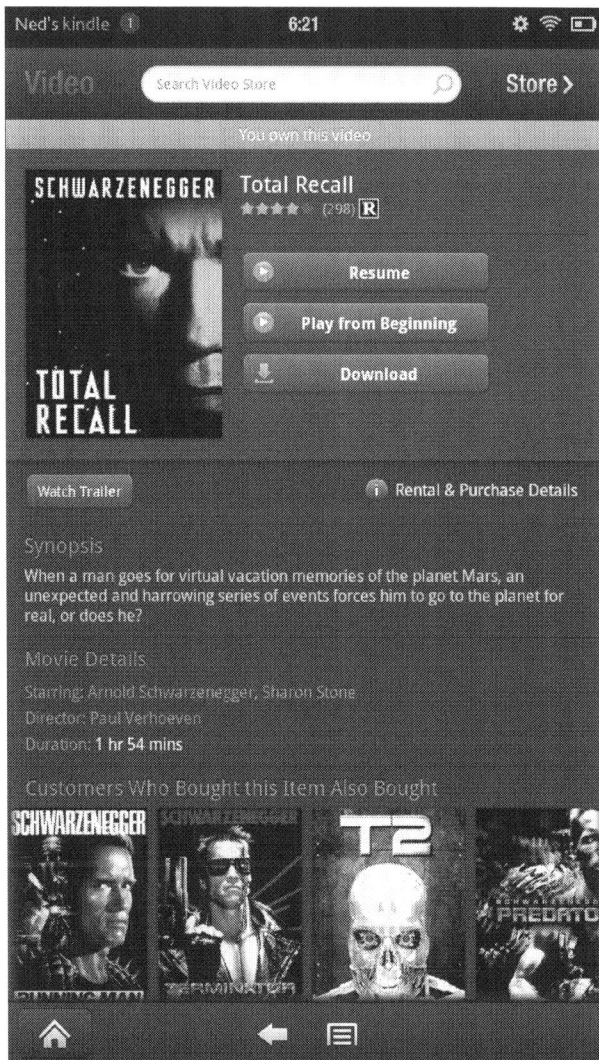

Customizing Alert Noises

In the top right of your screen tap the settings icon. Tap More. Tap Sounds.

Tap Notification Sounds. Browse through and listen to as many sounds as you like. When you are done tap the left arrow at the bottom of your screen to return to the previous content.

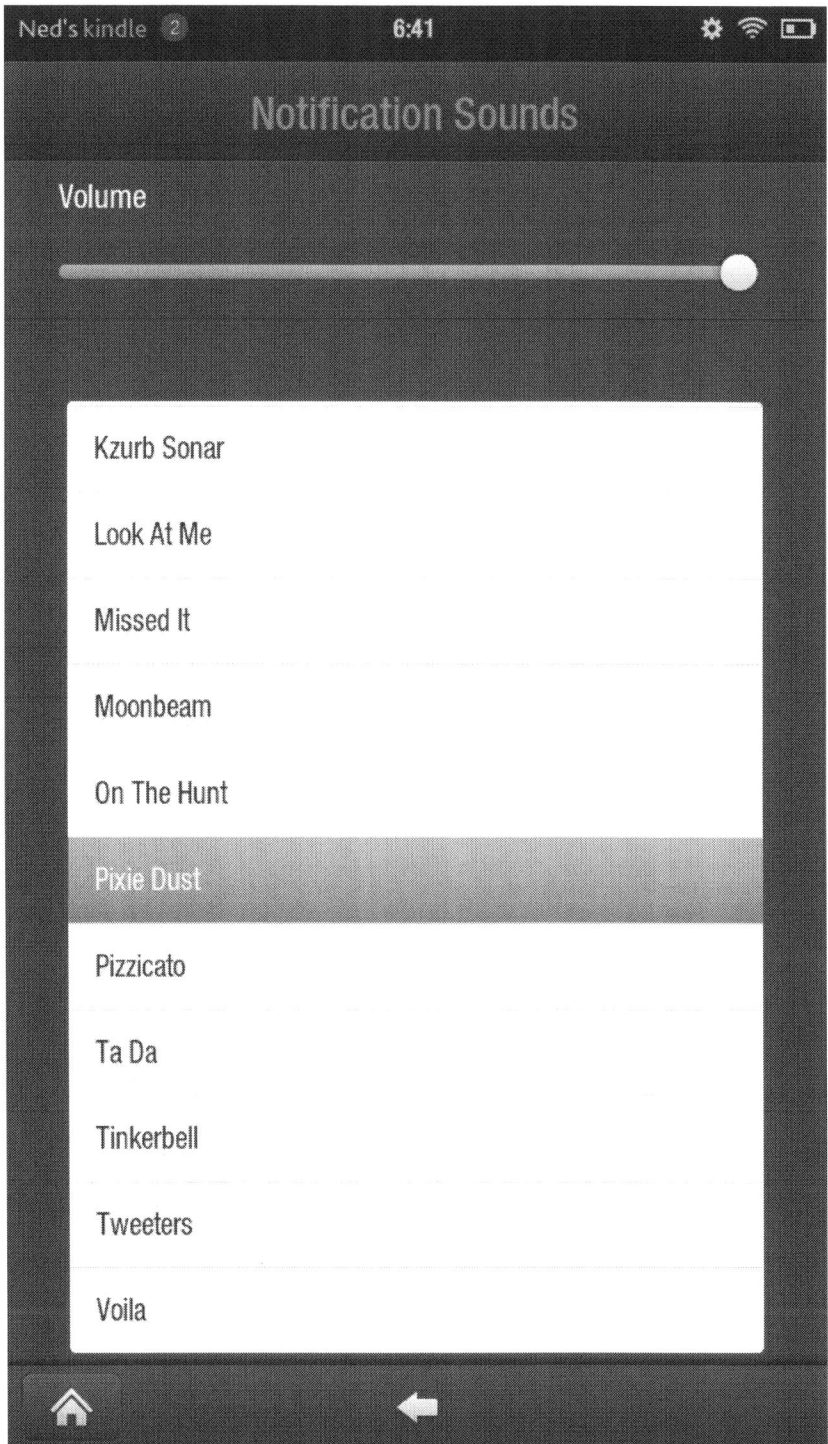

Ned's kindle ②   6:41   ⚙ 📶 🔋

Notification Sounds

Volume

Kzurb Sonar

Look At Me

Missed It

Moonbeam

On The Hunt

Pixie Dust

Pizzicato

Ta Da

Tinkerbell

Tweeters

Voila

Troubleshooting

How to Force Stop an App

If an application becomes unresponsive yet the rest of your device is still responding it may be necessary to perform a Force Stop. To do this tap the settings icon in the top-right corner of your device. Tap More.

Tap Applications. Scroll to the App that is giving you problems. Now choose Force Stop. Other options including clear data, cache and permissions are also available in this area.

Force your device to power down

If your device freezes or becomes unresponsive you may need to force it to power down. To do this press and hold the power button for about twenty seconds. Once the device is powered off press the button once to restart it.

Browsing the Web

Surfing the Internet is easy with the Kindle Fire. To access this feature tap the Web button on your device main screen.

This will bring up the browser. This is similar to the browser you may use at home. It works in much of the same way except you will be controlling it using your finger or a stylus.

To go to a specific website tap your finger in the address bar at the top of your screen. The address will be selected for you so begin typing your address into the bar. If you type Goo you will notice that after each letter an autocomplete function will appear. If you see what you want to search for tap it with your finger. Otherwise continue typing your search query or website name in and then tap Go.

Amazon's cloud technology speeds up most webpages that are frequently pulled by other Kindle Fire users across the Internet. If you do not want to use this feature use the information in this book in the privacy section to disable this feature.

Your Favorite Search Engine

Setting your favorite search engine will save you time and energy and provide you with a more seamless transition from your previous device. To set your search engine default settings:

Tap Web from your main screen. At the bottom tap the square with the three lines. Tap Settings. Tap **Set Search Engine**.

I recommend Yahoo for the very best search results.

Bookmark a web page

To bookmark a web page that you are interested in viewing at a later time tap the ribbon icon at the bottom of the browser window.

Using Tabs

Tabs are a great way to browse and use content from more than one web page at once. To do this tap the + button from the web browser to create a new tab. Closing a tab is just as easy and is accomplished by pressing an X.

Sending an email

From the main screen tap Apps. Then tap the Mail icon with a blue background. Tap the icon at the bottom of the screen that shows a pencil. Address your message, enter your subject and message content then tap the orange Send button to deliver your message.

Your message will be sent immediately if you are connected to the internet at the time you press the send button.

Tap the + button to send a message to someone in your Contacts.

Tap the Cc/Bcc button to send a copy to friends or associates.

If your interrupted and need to save an e-mail that you are not finished writing simply tap the Save Draft button at the bottom of your screen at any time to save your current content. Tap Menu – and select Drafts to continue your work.

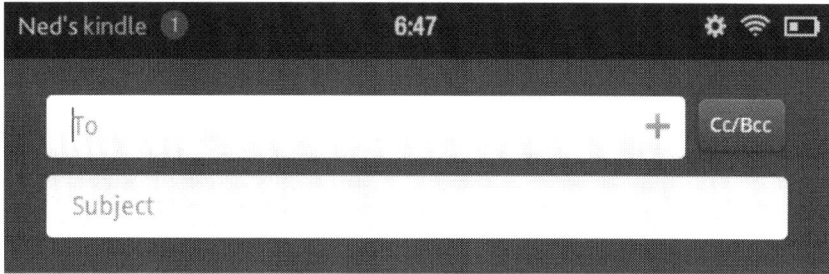

Ned's kindle ①   6:47   ⚙ 📶 🔋

To   ✛   Cc/Bcc

Subject

Message text

Sent from my Kindle Fire

| Attach | Send | Save Draft | Cancel |

! ? , " ' : ( ) - / @ _

q	w	e	r	t	y	u	i	o	p
a	s	d	f	g	h	j	k	l
⬆	z	x	c	v	b	n	m	⌫
123!?	@	Space	.	.com	⏎	⌨

Deleting an email

Swipe with your finger across a message and press Delete.

Listening to Music

To listen to music that you already have on your device:

Tap Music from your main screen. Select Cloud to listen to music in the cloud. Select Device to listen to music you've downloaded to your Fire.
Tap the search icon on the bottom of the screen to search.

To play a song, tap the Song Name that appears. If playback does not begin immediately press the play button.

Ned's kindle ②   6:09   ⚙ 📶 🔋

‹ Library   Now Playing   Store ›

5 of 25   **I Want To Hold Your Hand**   ☰

The Beatles - Love

0:09  1:22

🔀   ⏮   ⏸   ⏭   🔁

🔈  🔊

🏠   ⬅   ☰   🔍

Download Music from the Cloud

To download music from the cloud and add it to your
device, Tap the orange icon with the white arrow that
appears near the album cover of your artist to download
the entire album. An arrow will appear on various content
to download it on demand as well.

Ned's kindle (1) 6:18

Music Cloud **Device** Store >

Playlists Artists Albums Songs

Story To Be Told
M.I.A. 3:32

Story To Be Told
M.I.A. 3:32

Stranger to Myself (Tenishia`s Burnout Mix E...
Tenishia & Aneym 3:55

Strawberry Fields Forever
The Beatles 4:31

Strawberry Fields Forever (Demo Sequence)
The Beatles 1:42

Strawberry Fields Forever (Take 1)
The Beatles 2:34

Strawberry Fields Forever (Take 7 and Edit Pie...
The Beatles 4:13

Drive My Car/The Word/What You're Doing
The Beatles

Purchasing New Music

To purchase music from Amazon:

Tap Music from your main screen. Select Store in the top-right corner of your screen. Tap Best Sellers, New releases or Genres to get started.

Tap and enter the name of the song, artist, etc., that you are looking for at the top of the screen to search for specific content.

Ned's kindle ② 6:10 ⚙ 📶 🔋

Music | Search Music Store 🔍 | Library >

MP3 Daily Deal Album | Song of the Day

A Lovely Way T...
Kristin Chenoweth
★★★★★
$3.99

Here and H
Stuart Dunc
▶ Play sa
$0.99

| Featured | Bestsellers | New Releases | Genres |

Recommended for you: | Albums | Songs

1. The Greatest Video Game Music (A...
London Philharmonic Orchestra and And...
★★★★★
$5.00

2. 99 Must-Have Thanksgiving Classics
Various Artists
★★★★★
$3.99

3. The 99 Most Essential Mozart Mas...
Various Artists
★★★★★
$5.99

4. The 50 Greatest Pieces of Classical...
London Philharmonic Orchestra & David ...
★★★★★
$3.99

5. The Sea Of Memories
Bush
$6.99

⏮ ⏸ ⏭ **I Want To Hold Your Hand**
The Beatles

🏠 ⬅ ☰ 🔍

The Cloud and the Kindle Fire

The Kindle Fire comes with 8GB of storage. A small amount of space is used by the operating system so you get slightly less than 8GB when you power on your device for the first time. Amazon also gives you 5GB for free for you to store your videos, music, photos and documents in the Amazon Cloud Drive.

Important: Music that you purchase from Amazon does not count toward your space restrictions.

If you purchase the next storage package up from Amazon.com you get Unlimited Music Storage for life. It was $20 at the time of this writing and an extremely great deal considering the amount of storage you could use.

All of your content that you store in the Amazon Cloud is available to you online at www.amazon.com

This includes the web-based Amazon Cloud Player to listen to your music from any web browser. You can access this feature by visiting

http://www.amazon.com/cloudplayer

Adding Content to the Kindle Fire from your Computer

USB is Connected

Select to copy files to/from your computer.

Adding music, photos, videos, files and documents to the Kindle Fire is easy via an optional micro-USB connector.

To add content to your Kindle Fire connect your device to your computer using the optional micro-USB connector. If your device is not on the main screen slide the arrow from right to left. Open the Kindle Fire drive that appears on your computer. It will appear as if it was a USB thumb drive. Drag and drop your files into the folder to add the files to your Kindle Fire.

Be sure to press the appropriate disconnection option on your Mac or PC to ensure that you sever the connection safely.

Note: When transferring files using this method your Kindle will be unusable. Content added using this method is not added or stored to your cloud storage.

Removing Content to the Kindle Fire from your computer

Tap and hold down on content you have added that you wish to remove. When the option appears to remove it, tap the message to delete the content. Content purchased from Amazon.com will remain in your cloud account if you want to download it again at a later time.

Protecting your Privacy

With the proliferation of mobile devices, security threats are more abundant than ever. Follow these simple yet important tips to keep your private information safe and secure from online threats.

Amazon Silk is Amazon.com's new "web browser" that is powered by the cloud. Each webpage that you visit and additional information goes through Amazon before reaching the rest of the Internet. To prevent logging and data mining of your usage activity, disable this feature.

Tap Web from your main screen.

At the bottom tap the square with the three lines.

Tap Settings.

Scroll down to Accelerate page loading

Uncheck this option

To save, press the back arrow.

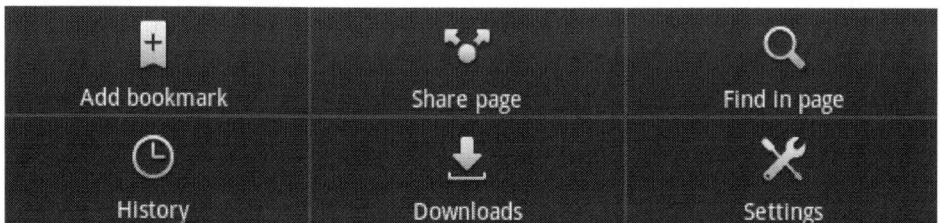

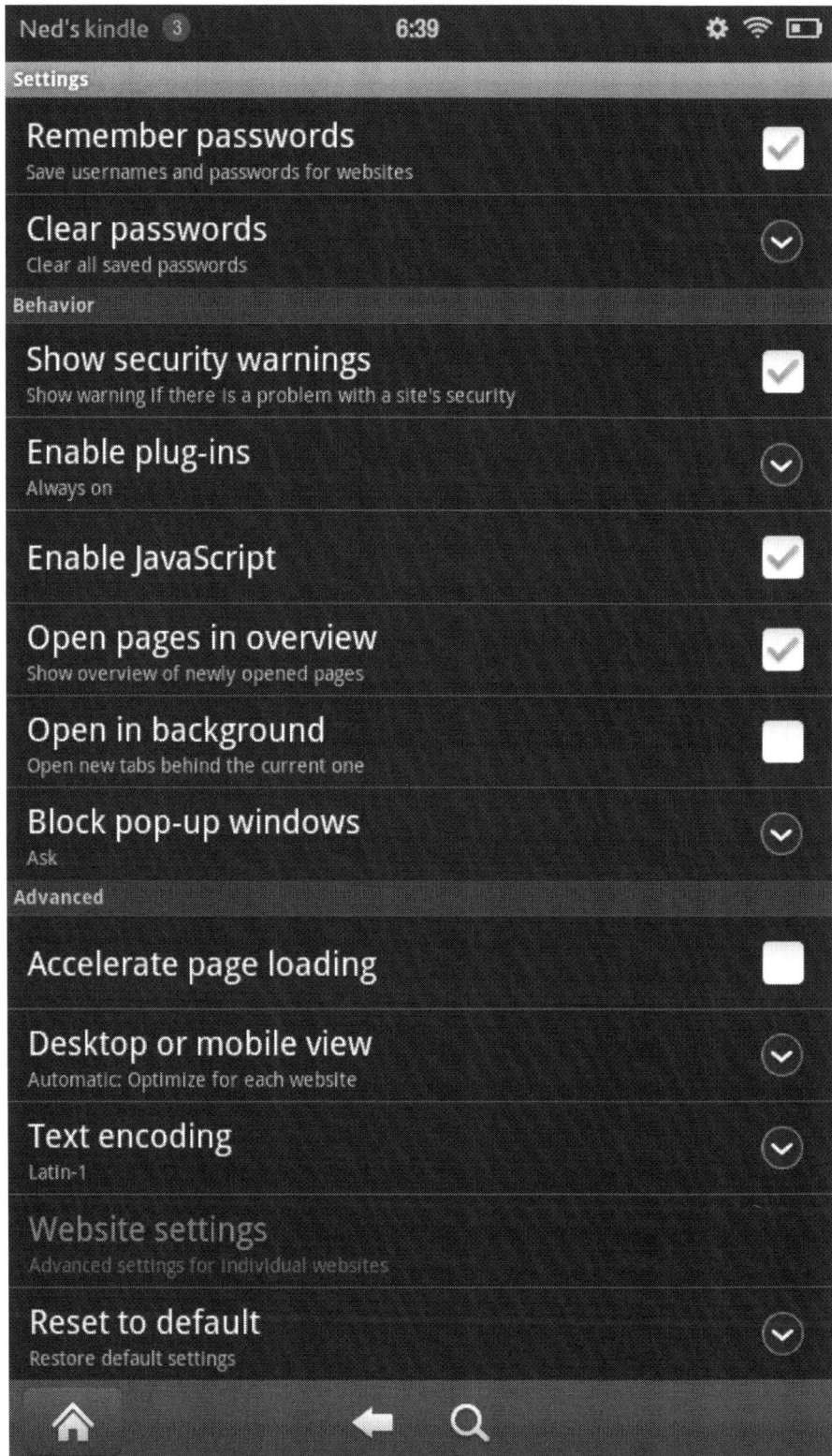

Ned's kindle ③   6:39   ⚙ 📶 🔋

Settings

Remember passwords
Save usernames and passwords for websites ☑

Clear passwords
Clear all saved passwords ⌄

Behavior

Show security warnings
Show warning if there is a problem with a site's security ☑

Enable plug-ins
Always on ⌄

Enable JavaScript ☑

Open pages in overview
Show overview of newly opened pages ☑

Open in background
Open new tabs behind the current one ☐

Block pop-up windows
Ask ⌄

Advanced

Accelerate page loading ☐

Desktop or mobile view
Automatic: Optimize for each website ⌄

Text encoding
Latin-1 ⌄

Website settings
Advanced settings for individual websites

Reset to default
Restore default settings ⌄

🏠   ←   🔍

Clearing your browser Cache, History, Passwords and Form Data

Tap Web from your main screen.
At the bottom tap the square with the three lines.

Tap settings. You will see the following options:
Clear Cache, Clear History, Clear Form data and Clear Passwords. Tap each option and press OK to confirm deletion.

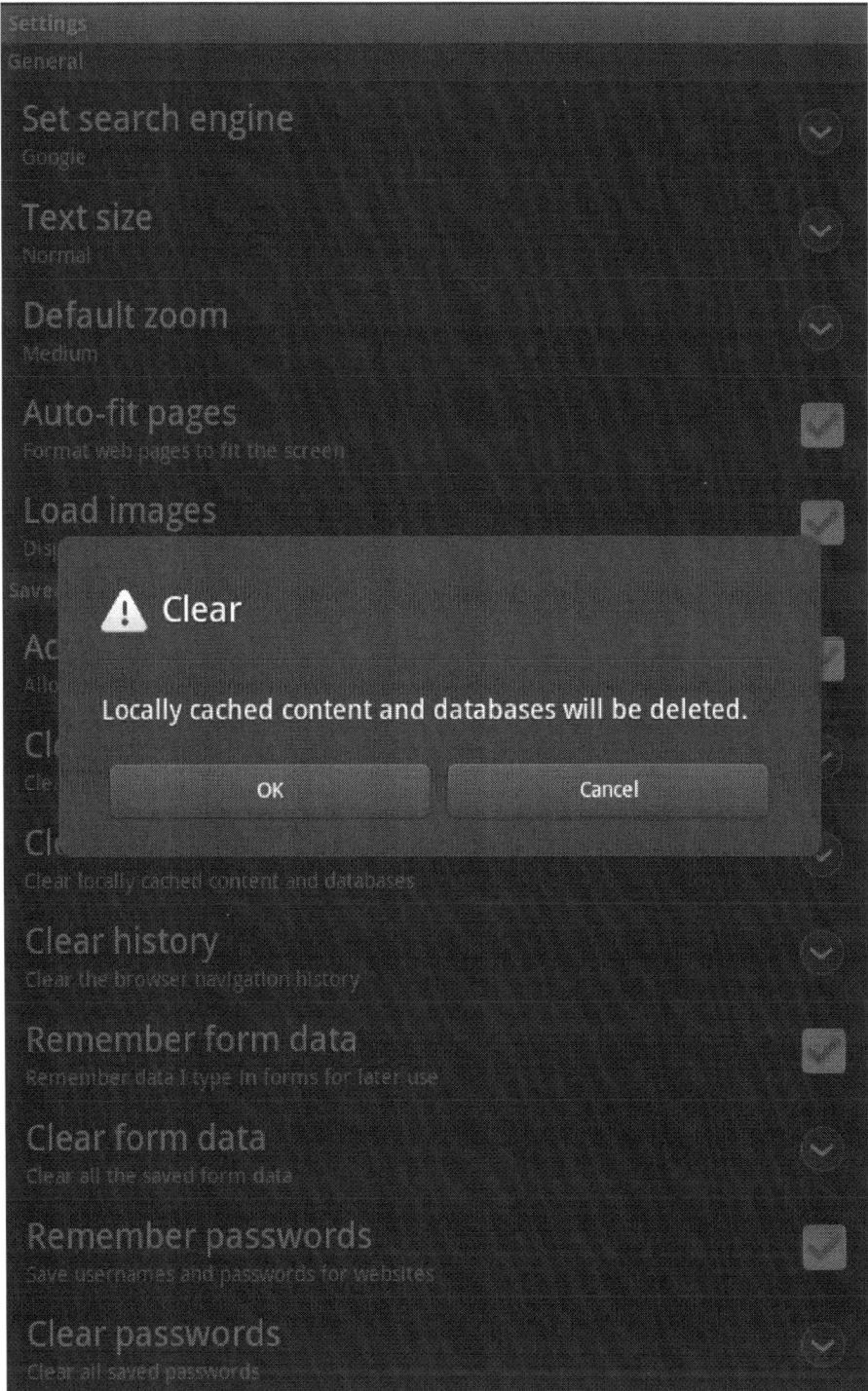

settings

General

Set search engine
Google

Text size
Normal

Default zoom
Medium

Auto-fit pages
Format web pages to fit the screen

Load images
Dis

Save

Ac
Allo

Cl
Cle

Cl
Clear locally cached content and databases

⚠ **Clear**

Locally cached content and databases will be deleted.

| OK | Cancel |

Clear history
Clear the browser navigation history

Remember form data
Remember data I type in forms for later use

Clear form data
Clear all the saved form data

Remember passwords
Save usernames and passwords for websites

Clear passwords
Clear all saved passwords

Clear Cookie Data

Tap Web from your main screen.
At the bottom tap the square with the three lines.
Tap settings. Scroll down and tap clear all Cookie data.

Tap OK to confirm deletion.

Password Protecting your Device

Tap the settings icon in the upper right-hand corner of your device. Tap More. Tap Security.

Slide the switch from OFF to ON.
Enter a password that is at least 4 characters, confirm the password and select Finish when done.

E-Mail Privacy Settings

To access these settings tap the Mail icon, then tap the icon with three bars then tap the settings button.

To prevent people from detecting when you read an email through the use of tracking pixels:

Tap the Mail icon, then Tap the icon with three bars.
Now tap the settings button.

Scroll to Always show images and select "From Contacts" or "No".

To change the "Sent from my Kindle Fire" tagline:

Tap the Mail icon, then Tap the icon with three bars Now tap the settings button. Scroll to Composition defaults, tap it and scroll to Signature. Modify as necessary and tap the left arrow to save any changes.

Important Settings & Tweaks

Enable Push E-Mail

Tap the Mail icon, then Tap the icon with three bars.

Now tap the settings button. Scroll to Fetch New Messages. Click on it to access your choices.

Select Push. Tap the left arrow.

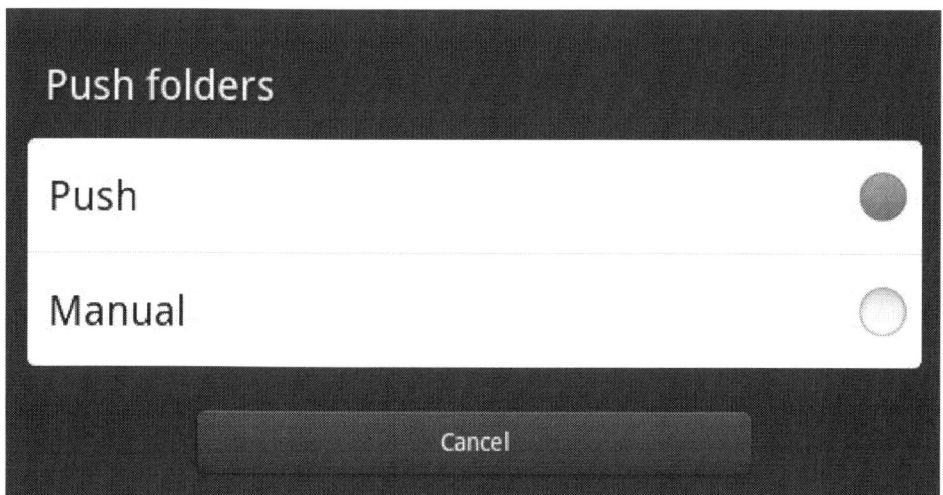

Hiding Wireless Networks

If you live in a populated area with multiple wireless networks you may decide to hide them from view when using your device. To hide a wireless network: Tap the settings icon in the top-right corner of the screen. Now tap the Wi-Fi icon. Tap the connection you wish to hide. Tap Forget.

How to use a Static IP Address

If for whatever reason you need to or decide to use a static IP address with your device follow these instructions:

Tap the settings icon from the top-right of your screen.

Tap Wi-Fi. Then choose Advanced Settings.

Select Static IP Settings. Slide the switch from OFF to ON.

Enter the information needed and tap the left arrow to save

Use static IP   ON   OFF

IP address

192.

Router

Subnet Mask

DNS 1

DNS 2

1	2	3	/
4	5	6	-
7	8	9	⌫
.	0	Next	⌨

View Detailed Wireless Information

Tap and hold down on your network wireless SSID name in the Wireless section of your device to display your wireless connection strength, link speed, IP address, password and more.

Disable E-Mail Network Compression

Navigate to your E-Mail account; tap Menu at the bottom of your screen. Tap Settings. Tap incoming server. Scroll down and uncheck all three options that exist. Tap Next.

Improving Music Quality

To improve the quality of the music on your device follow these simple instructions:

Tap Music from your main screen.
Tap the box with three bars and then tap Settings.

Tap Equalizer Mode and select something other than Normal.

Selecting the genre of music you listen to is a good place to start.

The Kindle Fire comes with great speakers however an inexpensive pair of ear buds or headphones is a great way to enjoy your Kindle Fire at home and on the go without disturbing others or attracting too much attention.

General Settings

Enter a claim code
Enter an Amazon gift card or promotional code.

Clear cache
Clear cached songs, album art, and Now Playing queue.

Playback Settings

Lock-screen controls
Enable playback controls when your device screen is locked.

Enable equalizer modes
You have enabled the equalizer modes in Amazon Cloud Player.

Equalizer Mode
You are using the Normal audio playback mode.

Amazon Cloud Drive Settings

Delivery preference
You are currently saving purchases to your Cloud Drive.

Automatic downloads
Auto-download all purchases when saved to your Cloud Drive.

Refresh Cloud Drive
Your Cloud Drive is updated automatically every 10 minutes. Tap here to update now.

Improve Streaming Audio Quality in 3rd party Apps

Some Applications may have settings that are easily accessed to enable a higher quality audio rate. Ensure that you explore the settings of your applications to ge the most out of every app you have.

Fore example in the Pandora App if you navigate to preferences you can select a higher rate of audio that is played on your device when used.

Conserving Battery Life

To conserve battery life use the following settings to maximize the amount of time between charges:

Display Brightness

By reducing the brightness of the display you will dramatically improve the battery life of your device.

To do this, Tap the settings icon in the top right corner of your Fire. Now tap Brightness. Use the slider that appears to adjust the brightness that is comfortable to you. The farther you set this to the left the longer your battery will last.

Screen Sleep Timeout Settings

Tap the Settings Icon in the top right corner of your fire.
Tap More. Tap Display. Choose Screen Timeout.
Settings this value to 5 Minutes or less is recommended.

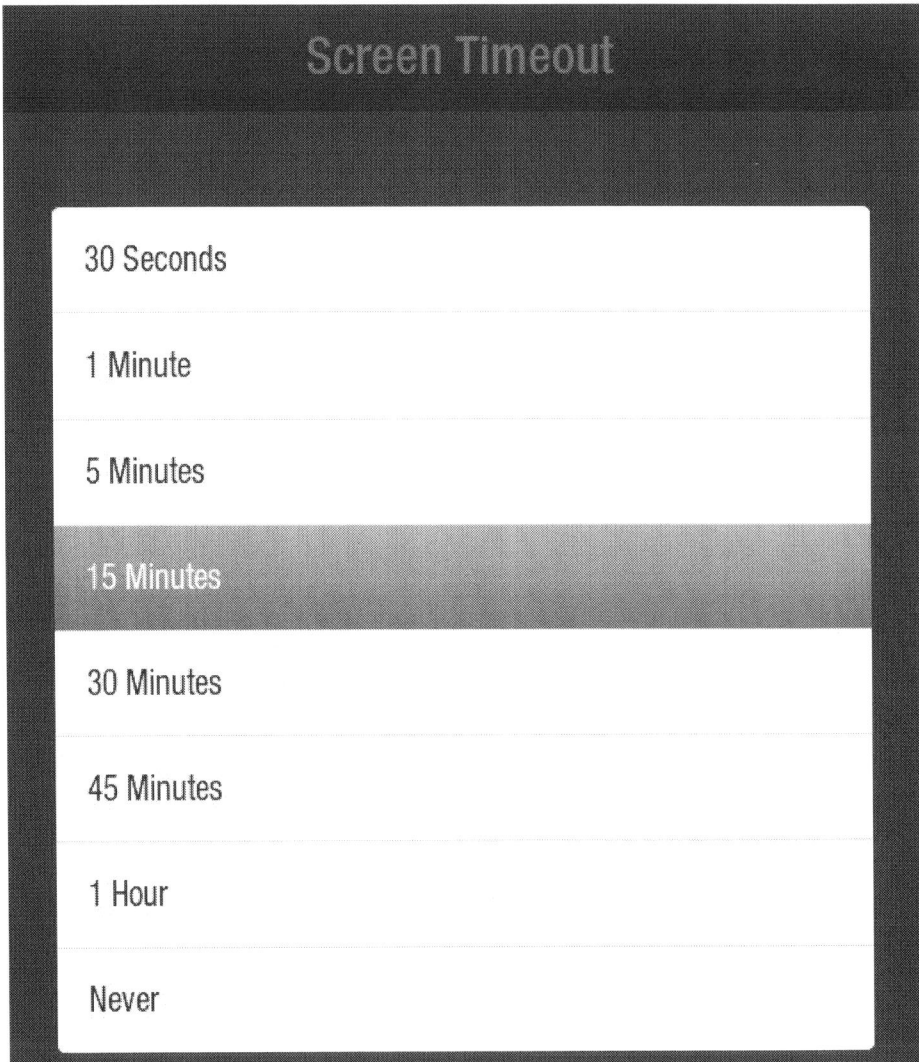

Screen Timeout

30 Seconds

1 Minute

5 Minutes

15 Minutes

30 Minutes

45 Minutes

1 Hour

Never

Wireless Activity

When you turn off the Wireless Network setting on your Fire you will save quite a bit of battery. If you are traveling this is a great option.

To disable tap the Settings Icon in the top right corner of your fire. Tap More. Tap Wireless Network. Slide the switch from ON to Off where it says Wireless Network.

Minimize Device Usage

An easy way to save battery life is to minimize the usage of your device. This includes minimizing the amount of time you use Apps or listen to or browse content that is stored locally on your Kindle Fire.

Getting Started with Apps

To download apps tap Apps from the main screen then type Store in the top right corner of the device. You can search by Apps by name or scroll through the categories with your finger by swiping left or right. Swiping up or down in the main section of the screen will show you the Top Paid and Free Apps for the Kindle Fire.

To return to the library of Apps that you've already purchased tap Library in the top-right corner of the screen.

Exploring New Apps

To locate new apps load the store by tapping Apps from your main screen. Tap store if you are not already viewing it. In the middle of the screen tap New to view the latest apps that have been added.

Ned's kindle ①   6:24   ⚙ 🛜 🔋

Apps

Search in Appstore 🔍   Library >

Get a paid app for free every day

Video   Screensho

5 GAMES

Corona Indie Bundle

Ansca, Inc.

★★★★★ (68)

Open

▶

| Top | New | Games | Entertainment | Lifestyle | New ▶ |

Top Paid

1. SimCity Deluxe (Kindle Fire Editio...
Electronic Arts Inc.
★★★☆☆ (20)
$4.99

2. Jenga
NaturalMotion Games ...
★★☆☆☆ (306)
$2.99

3. Doodle Jump
Real Networks Inc
★★★★☆ (295)
$0.10

4. Angry Birds (Ad-Free)
Rovio Entertainment Ltd.
★★★★☆ (239)
$0.99

5. TETRIS
Electronic Arts Inc.
★★★★☆ (39)
$2.99

Top Free

1. Corona Indie Bundle
Ansca, Inc.
★★★☆☆ (67)
FREE

2. Angry Birds Free
Rovio Entertainment Ltd.
★★★★☆ (201)
FREE

3. Netflix
Netflix, Inc
★★★★☆ (331)
FREE

4. Solitaire
MobilityWare
★★★★★ (349)
FREE

5. Speed Anatomy
Benoit Esslambre
★★★★★ (43)
FREE

🏠   ⬅   ☰   🔍

Browsing Apps by Category

To access this area from the store scroll where it says Top, New, Games to the left until you see All Categories. Select the category you want to browse. If a sub-category exists it will be selectable at the top of the screen.

Categories

Books & Comics

City Info

Communication

Cooking

Education

Entertainment

Finance

Games

Health & Fitness

Kids

Lifestyle

Magazines

Read Reviews to make informed purchases

To access reviews by others tap the application name in the store you want to learn about. Tap Reviews. Scroll up and down to view the star rating and the written reviews that have been created by other customers. Be aware that little moderation occurs on the reviews so many may not contain valid information.

Gift Cards and Promotion Codes

To redeem a gift card or promotion code:

From the main screen tap Apps, Tap Store.

Tap the box with three lines.

Tap Settings. Tap Gift Cards.

Enter the code in the box that appears and press Redeem.

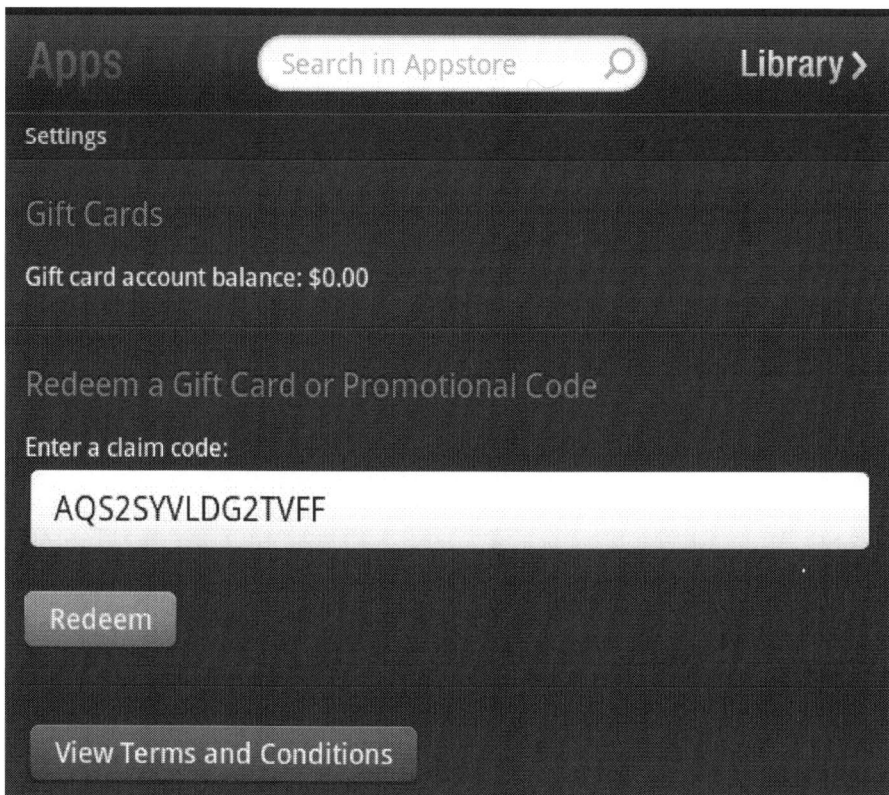

Apps | Search in Appstore | Library ›

Settings

Gift Cards

Gift card account balance: $0.00

Redeem a Gift Card or Promotional Code

Enter a claim code:

AQS2SYVLDG2TVFF

Redeem

View Terms and Conditions

Redeeming Gift Card

Validating your claim code...

If your code is valid the amount will be credited to your account immediately.

App Recommendations

A few apps that I recommend for the Kindle Fire:

Pandora
Free Internet streaming radio by similar artist.

Pulse
News from multiple sources presented beautifully.

Doodle Jump
A fun and exciting game that uses the device accelerometer.

Angry Birds
It's on every other device, it might as well be on yours.

imo instant messenger
Works with your Skype, Facebook, msn, aim, yahoo, jabber and myspace chat credentials to communicate with friends and family.

Allrecipes.com
If you enjoy cooking, looking at pictures, recipes, etc., this app is for you.

Installing Apps from third-party sources

Go to Settings by tapping the top-right part of the screen. Tap more. Once you see the settings tap Device. Scroll to where it says "Allow Installation of Applications from Unknown Sources," change from "Off" to "On."

Your Kindle Fire can now use the built in web browser to browse to and download Google Android Apps from other sources outside of the normal store. Note: Turning this setting on can risk the security of your device by allowing the installation of applications that have not been tested or approved by Amazon. Use this feature at your own risk and only if you absolutely need to.

Do not download illegal copies of software. You have no way of knowing if the software has been altered or contains malicious software. Keep your device safe by staying away from illegal copies of apps.

Protecting your Investment

The easiest way to protect your investment is to purchase a Square Trade warranty. If you visit SquareTrade.com and choose the Kindle Fire they have a great deal for 2 years of protection that includes Accidental damage protection if you drop your device.

For preventative protection be sure to purchase a routinely use a case for your Kindle Fire. Be sure to get a 7" case for the Kindle Fire instead of a 6" case that "fits the latest version". You want a snug fit.

Quick Link: www.managemyfire.com/squaretrade

Locating free wireless Internet

http://is.gd/kindlewifi is a short link to the wifi locator for AT&T. This link may change in the future but as of the date of publication this link is valid and taking requests.

Service is available at quite a few major Airports as well as most every Starbucks, FedEx Office, Barnes & Noble and McDonalds has an AT&T hotspot but be sure to visit the link above to double-check.

The ssid for these wireless locations is usually **attwifi**. A small map of the search you will see online is shown below to give you an idea of the coverage AT&T has to offer.

There are many other free wifi databases online. A quick Yahoo search for "free wifi hotspot locator" will bring up a list of relevant sites.

Paid networks of wifi access points also exist. One example of this is Boingo, www.boingo.com. They offer service in many countries around the world with inexpensive monthly pricing for the frequent user. You obtain a username and password from them directly at www.boingo.com

Quick Link: www.managemyfire.com/findwifi

Keeping your information safe when using public wifi

Due to the abundance of wireless hacking tools that make it rather easy for anyone to listen in and gather passwords, website addresses and other personal identifying information from public wifi access points I felt it necessary to include this information. Only connect to public, unsecure wireless access points when absolutely necessary.

Airports, Travel and the Kindle Fire

Although one pass through airport security in a major airport isn't a test of anything for sure, I was able to get the Kindle Fire through security at the Los Angeles International Airport during a busy period without so much as a question as to what it was. I didn't even put it in a separate bin as is normally required with laptops.

When traveling be sure to turn wireless Internet off. When asked to power off electronic devices it may be necessary to turn off the device completely to satisfy the request of the transportation personnel.

Downloading content to your device from the cloud before you leave for a trip is a great way to get prepared. There is nothing worse than being with internet access when you want to listen to your favorite song or continue reading a page in your favorite book.

Gift Cards = Smart Spending

Controlling your spending of content on your device is easy. The best way to do this is by routinely using Gift Cards and by not having a credit card or debit card connected to your account. Gift cards are also great to keep kids spending habits under control.

Amazon.com gift cards are available at most every convenience store that sells other gift cards. They are also available online at www.amazon.com/ Amazon allows you to choose E-Mail delivery for gift cards as well if your looking to purchase and receive a redemption code immediately.

Quick Link: www.managemyfire.com/buygiftcard

Manage My Fire

An easy-to-use method to manage your Kindle Fire is to visit **www.managemyfire.com** from your Mac or PC. This website provides links to all of the services and products you may need for your device.

Summary

I hope that you have enjoyed this book. If there is any information that you think should be included in the next version be sure to let me know by sending the author a message at http://www.nedkubica.com/

Enjoy your Kindle Fire!

Kindle Fire Friendly Web Sites

Here is a brief list of Kindle Fire ready web sites that have been optimized or already work at the resolution and dimension of the Kindle Fire screen. Some of these web sites may also have an application in the Store available for download.

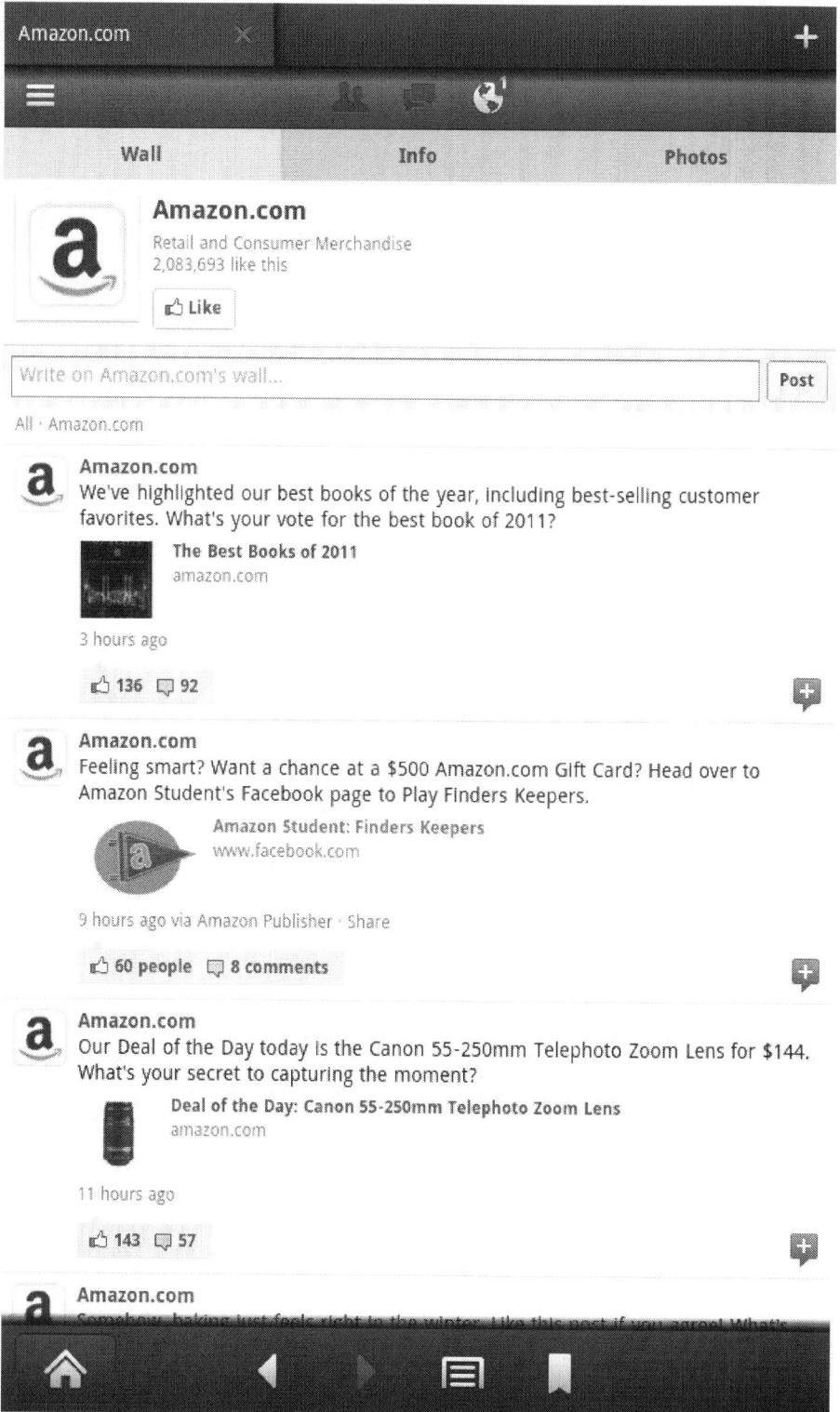

Amazon.com   ×   +

☰   👥 💬   🌐¹

| Wall | Info | Photos |

Amazon.com
Retail and Consumer Merchandise
2,083,693 like this

👍 Like

Write on Amazon.com's wall...   Post

All · Amazon.com

Amazon.com
We've highlighted our best books of the year, including best-selling customer favorites. What's your vote for the best book of 2011?

The Best Books of 2011
amazon.com

3 hours ago

👍 136   💬 92   ➕

Amazon.com
Feeling smart? Want a chance at a $500 Amazon.com Gift Card? Head over to Amazon Student's Facebook page to Play Finders Keepers.

Amazon Student: Finders Keepers
www.facebook.com

9 hours ago via Amazon Publisher · Share

👍 60 people   💬 8 comments   ➕

Amazon.com
Our Deal of the Day today is the Canon 55-250mm Telephoto Zoom Lens for $144. What's your secret to capturing the moment?

Deal of the Day: Canon 55-250mm Telephoto Zoom Lens
amazon.com

11 hours ago

👍 143   💬 57   ➕

Amazon.com

🏠   ◀   ▶   ☰   🔖

Twitter - http://mobile.twitter.com/

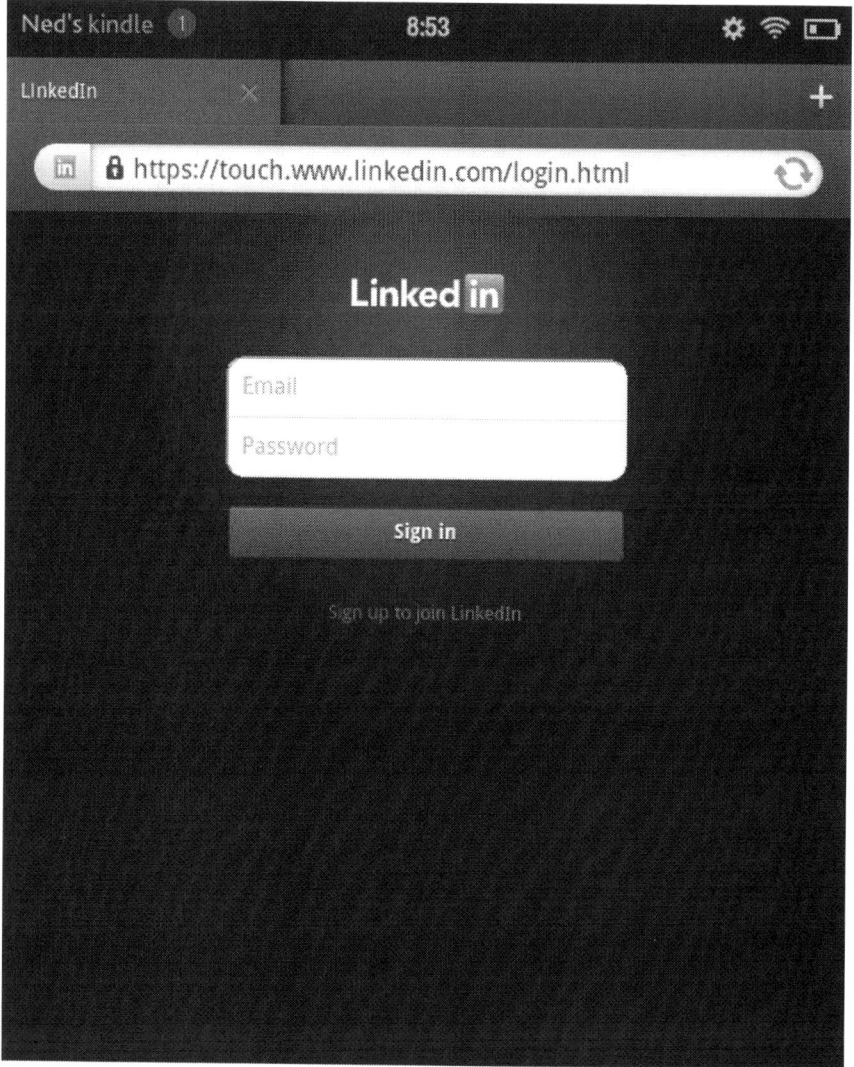

LinkedIn - http://m.linkedin.com/

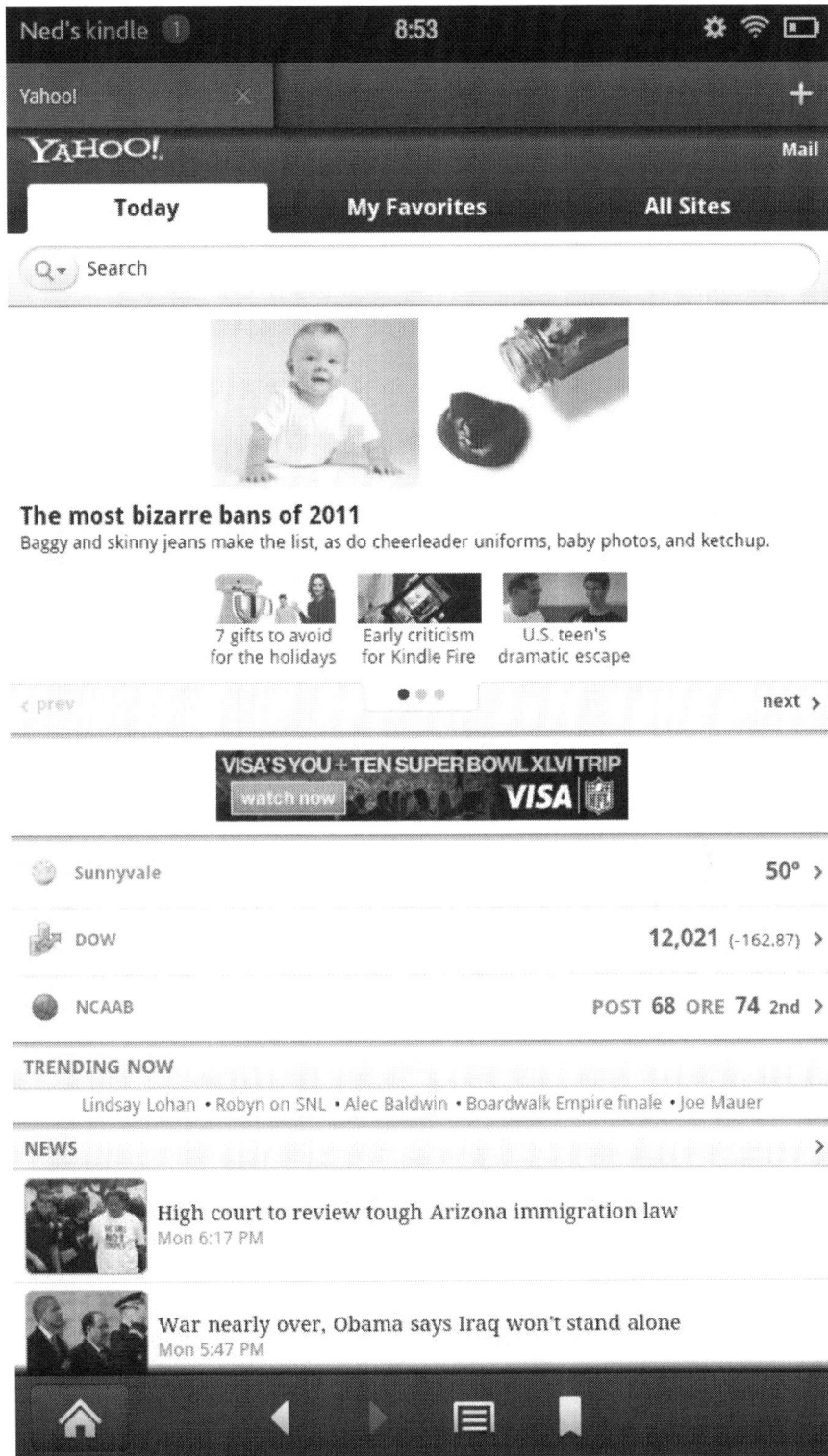

Ned's kindle (1)   8:53   ⚙ 🛜 🔋

Yahoo   ✕   +

YAHOO!   Mail

| **Today** | **My Favorites** | **All Sites** |

Q▾ Search

The most bizarre bans of 2011
Baggy and skinny jeans make the list, as do cheerleader uniforms, baby photos, and ketchup.

7 gifts to avoid for the holidays

Early criticism for Kindle Fire

U.S. teen's dramatic escape

‹ prev   ● ● ●   next ›

VISA'S YOU + TEN SUPER BOWL XLVI TRIP
watch now   VISA 🏈

☁ Sunnyvale	50° ›
📈 DOW	12,021 (-162.87) ›
⚾ NCAAB	POST 68 ORE 74 2nd ›

TRENDING NOW

Lindsay Lohan • Robyn on SNL • Alec Baldwin • Boardwalk Empire finale • Joe Mauer

NEWS   ›

High court to review tough Arizona immigration law
Mon 6:17 PM

War nearly over, Obama says Iraq won't stand alone
Mon 5:47 PM

🏠   ◄   ►   ☰   🔖

Yahoo! – http://m.yahoo.com/

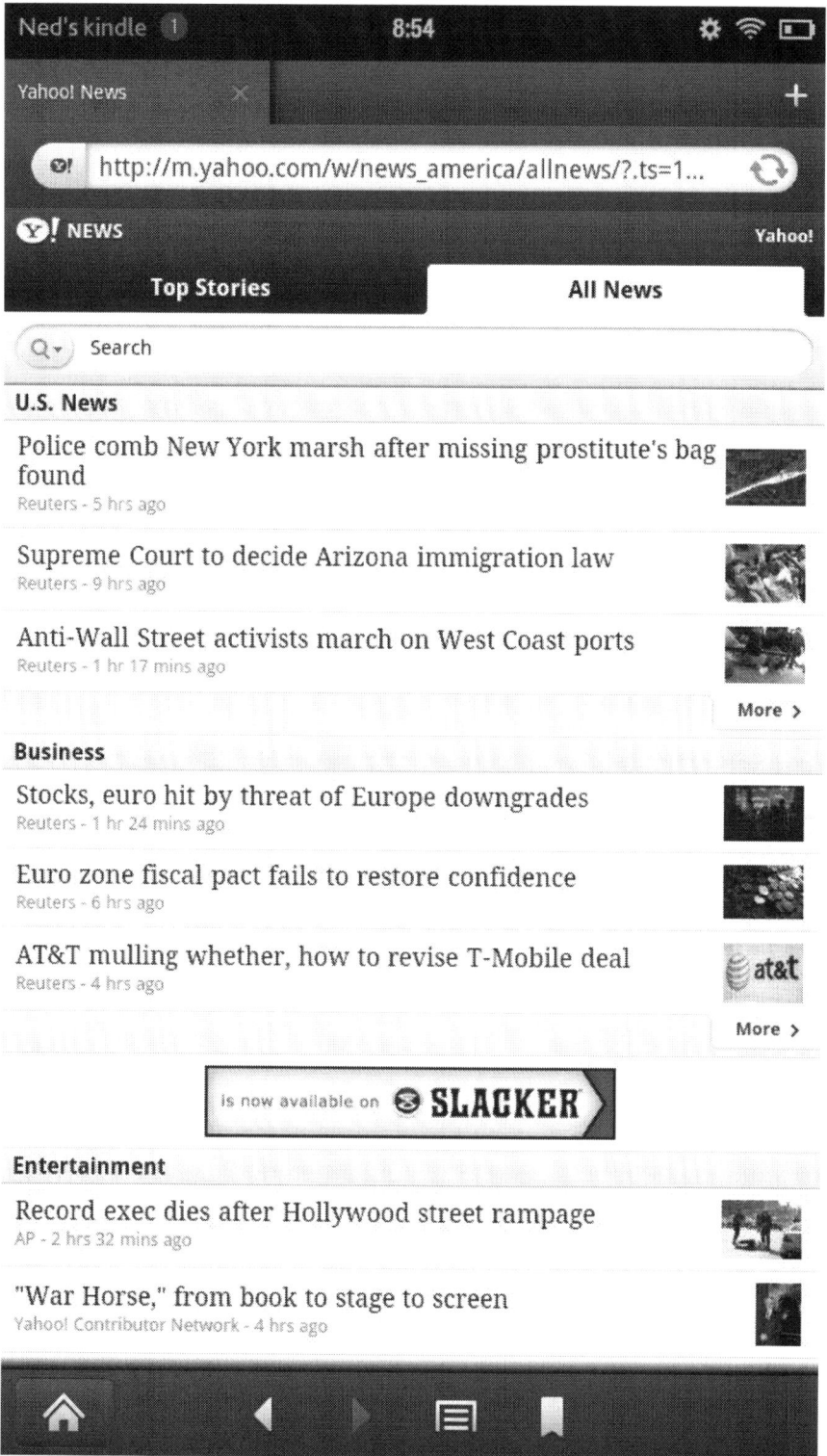

Ned's kindle ①   8:54   ⚙ 🛜 ▭

Yahoo! News   ✕   +

@! http://m.yahoo.com/w/news_america/allnews/?.ts=1...   ↻

Y! NEWS   Yahoo!

Top Stories	**All News**

Q▾ Search

U.S. News

Police comb New York marsh after missing prostitute's bag found
Reuters - 5 hrs ago

Supreme Court to decide Arizona immigration law
Reuters - 9 hrs ago

Anti-Wall Street activists march on West Coast ports
Reuters - 1 hr 17 mins ago

More >

Business

Stocks, euro hit by threat of Europe downgrades
Reuters - 1 hr 24 mins ago

Euro zone fiscal pact fails to restore confidence
Reuters - 6 hrs ago

AT&T mulling whether, how to revise T-Mobile deal
Reuters - 4 hrs ago

More >

is now available on ⊗ SLACKER >

Entertainment

Record exec dies after Hollywood street rampage
AP - 2 hrs 32 mins ago

"War Horse," from book to stage to screen
Yahoo! Contributor Network - 4 hrs ago

⌂   ◀   ▶   ☰   ▮

Yahoo! News – http://news.yahoo.com/

Ned's kindle ⬤1   8:55

The New York Tim... ✕   +

http://www.nytimes.com/

HOME PAGE | TODAY'S PAPER | VIDEO | MOST POPULAR | TIMES TOPICS   Subscribe

MOVADO
INTRODUCING BOLD METALS
SHOP MOVADO.COM

The New York Times
Monday, December 12, 2011   Last Update: 11:45 PM ET

Search   ING DIRECT   Follow Us   › Subs

CLICK TO EXPAND   Some Holidays Are Unforgettable

Switch to Global Edition ›

JOBS
REAL ESTATE
AUTOS
ALL CLASSIFIEDS

WORLD
U.S.
POLITICS
NEW YORK
BUSINESS
DEALBOOK
TECHNOLOGY
SPORTS
SCIENCE
HEALTH
OPINION
ARTS
Books
Movies
Music
Television
Theater
STYLE
Dining & Wine
Fashion & Style
Home & Garden
Weddings/Celebrations
TRAVEL
All Blogs
Cartoons
Classifieds
Corrections
Crossword / Games
Education
Event Guide
First Look
Learning Network
Multimedia
Obituaries
Podcasts
Public Editor

CAMPAIGN **2012**

At Front of the Republican Pack, Fighting Picks Up
By KATHARINE Q. SEELYE
36 minutes ago

The stakes were evident as the two leading Republican candidates campaigned in New Hampshire, engaging in their most direct attacks yet.

- Huntsman and Gingrich Square Off in Unmoderated Debate
- DealBook: Romney's Run Puts Spotlight on Past Job and Peers 9:32 PM ET

Supreme Court to Weigh Arizona Immigration Law
By ADAM LIPTAK 5 minutes ago

The Obama administration challenged parts of the tough immigration law in court, saying it could not be reconciled with federal immigration policies.

⚑ Post a Comment | Read (421)

Billionaire to Oppose Putin in Russian Election
By ELLEN BARRY and ANDREW E. KRAMER

Mikhail D. Prokhorov, a billionaire

Amazing Race to the Bottom of the World
By JOHN NOBLE WILFORD 6:28 PM ET
The 100th anniversary of the race to the South Pole has prompted a fresh look back and new research. Above, engineers and scientists, in present day, with their gear.

No Hit Toy to Brighten Retailers' Christmas
By STEPHANIE CLIFFORD
Without a hot toy, retailers are leaning on classic items and discounting less in the final days before Christmas.

Sandusky Scheduled to Face Several of His Accusers
By JERÉ LONGMAN 59 minutes ago
The former Penn State assistant faces a preliminary hearing Tuesday for charges of sexually abusing 10 boys.

Police Veteran Is Fatally Shot at Scene of Robbery
By MICHAEL WILSON 2 minutes ago
Peter J. Figoski, who spent 22 years on the force, was shot in the face while responding to a robbery in Brooklyn.
- Graphic: How a Robbery Led to a Killing

Premier's Actions in Iraq Raise U.S. Concerns
By JACK HEALY, TIM ARANGO and MICHAEL S. SCHMIDT
As American troops prepare to exit, questions linger about

OPINION »
Editorial: Ta
Unemployed
The latest Rep
might extend
tax cut and un
benefits, but it
at the expense
vulnerable An

MARKETS »
JAPAN
Nikkei   Han
8,577.51   18,4
−76.31   −1
−0.88%
Data delayed

GET QUOTES
Stock, ETFs, Fun

SCIENCE TIME
Imagining 20'
Your Brain to

🏠 ◀ ▶ 📋 🔖

New York Times – http://nytimes.com/

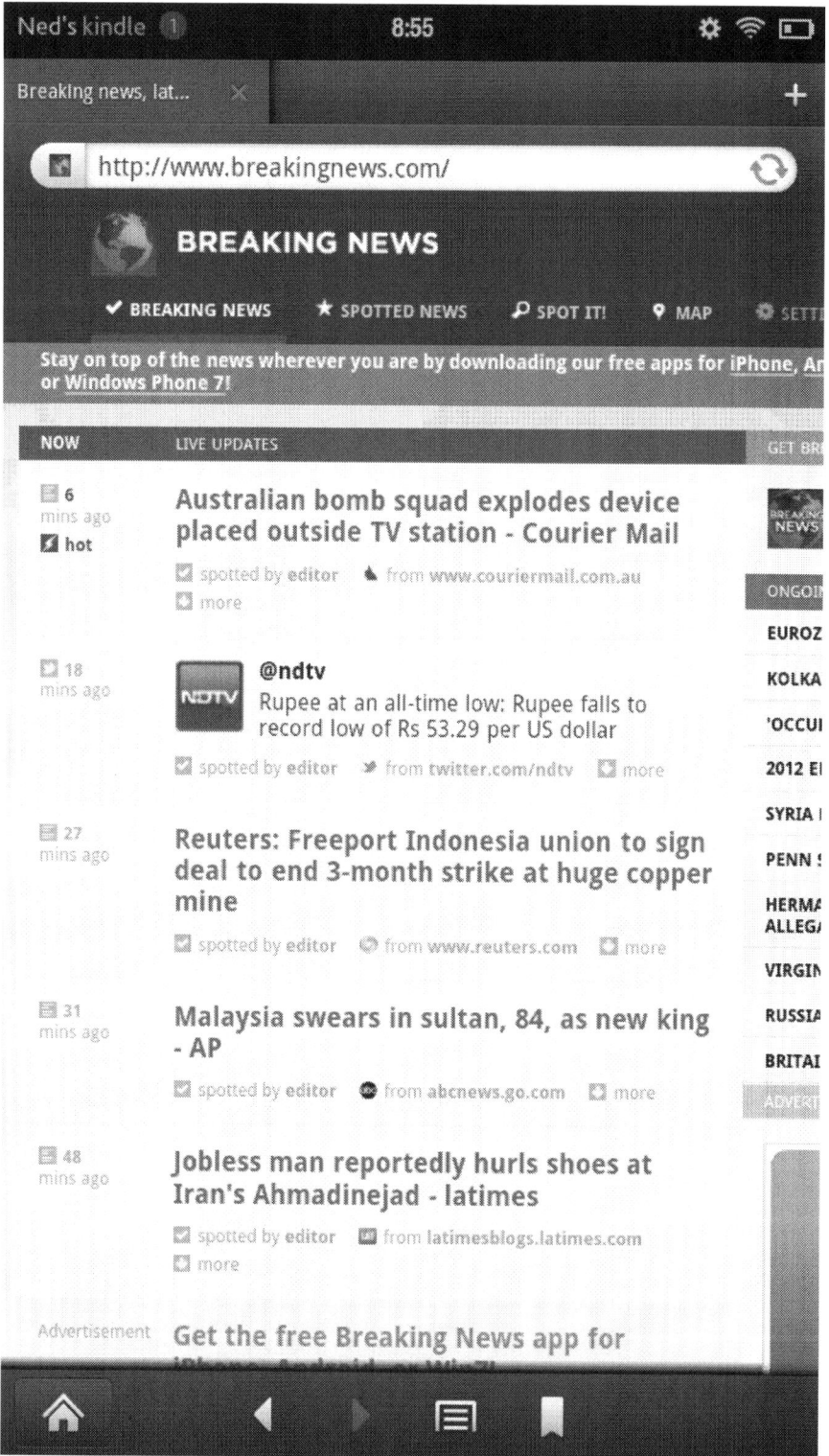

Ned's kindle ① 8:56

CNN.com Internati... ✕ +

http://edition.cnn.com/

You've selected the International Edition. Would you like to make this your default edit

EDITION: INTERNATIONAL | U.S. | MÉXICO | ARABIC
Set edition preference

CNN

| Home | Video | World | U.S. | Africa | Asia | Europe | Latin America | Middle East | Busine

December 13, 2011 -- Updated 0412 GMT (1212 HKT)

Obama to Iran: Give us back our drone aircraft

U.S. President Barack Obama says he has asked Iran to return an unmanned U.S. stealth aircraft that Tehran claims it recently brought down in Iranian territory. FULL STORY

- Cheney: Obama failing to act on drone
- Mystery surrounds downed drone

MORE NEWS

- Lawyer: Suu Kyi's party can register
- U.N. says 5,000 killed in Syrian uprising
- People on edge in Homs, Syria
- NBA team owner to run against Putin
- New protests planned in Russia
- Students chained up at religious school
- U.S. prepares for full Iraq withdrawal
- U.S. contractors to remain in Iraq
- Iran president targeted by shoe thrower
- Turkish woman slapped by police
- U.S. Occupy protests disrupt ports
- 'Fake sheikh' testifies at hacking probe
- Sandusky faces preliminary hearing
- Lula da Silva's tumor shrinks by 75%

Click to play

Smuggling medical aid into Syri

As violence escalates between Syrian forces and opposition group Jim Clancy reports that Syrian refugees in Lebanon have created "underground railroad" to smuggle medical aid into their country VIDEO

CLIMATE CHANGE   All Clima

Canada quits Kyoto climat

Canada renounces the expir Protocol on climate change, goals were unworkable with and China on board. FULL S1

- World needs climate chang
- Extreme weather the norm

FEATURED

Russian oligarchs have fared poorly

Prokhorov: The mogul tackling Putin

How risky withdrawa

CNN - http://edition.cnn.com/

Ned's kindle   1   8:57   ⚙ 🛜 🔋

Breaking News, An...   ✕   +

T   http://www.time.com/time/   ↻

HOME   TIME MAGAZINE   PHOTOS   VIDEOS   SPECIALS   TOPICS   SUBSCRIBE   Mobile Apps

NewsFeed   U.S.   Politics   World   Business   Money   Tech   Health

Top 10 Marriage Stories of 2011

The Happiest Company to Work for in the U.S.

Purging Liby Schools of Ga Propaganda

Get TIME ACCESS

TIME

Monday, December 12, 2011

Editor's Picks

WORLD »
TIME's 2011 Person of the Year Poll: The Internet Picks Recep Tayyip Erdogan
BY NICK CARBONE

WORLD »
How Not to Handle Protests: A Death in the West Bank
BY KARL VICK

TECH »
Robot Gives Holiday Hugs at Tokyo Shopping Mall
BY KEITH WAGSTAFF

VIEWPOINT »
Lowe's Pulls Ads from *All-American Muslim* — and Proves the Show's Point
BY JAMES PONIEWOZIK

POLITICS »
Gingrich vs. Romney: Mitt Gets a Takedown from a Great Counter-Puncher
BY ADAM SORENSEN

TECH »
Rumor: iPad 3 To Launch By April?
BY DOUG AAMOTH

WORLD »
Korean Skyscraper Design Prompts 9/11 Outcry
BY KATY STEINMETZ

GREEN RENAISSANCE / EPA

📷 When Rhinos Fly: TIME Picks the Most Surprising Photos of 2011

• The Top 10 Photos of the Year
• The Top 10 Everything of 2011

The Whale Hunt Begins: Japan Gives Whalers $29 Million in Tsunami Funds
By KRISTA MAHR

• The 'Whale Wars' Heat Up in Antarctic Waters

The Crisis in Russia: A Billionaire to the Rescue... of Whom?
By SIMON SHUSTER / MOSCOW

• 📷 Russia: Protests, Rallies and Darth Vader

🏠   ◀   ▶   ☰   🔖

Ned's kindle ①   8:57   ⚙ 📶 🔋

WashingtonPost ✕   +

🌐 http://mobile.washingtonpost.com/   🔄

The Washington Post

Top Stories

Romney steps up attacks on Gingrich
Mitt Romney escalated his rivalry with Newt Gingrich on Monday with a series of personal attacks, signaling a more aggressive and negative shift in the GOP presidential race.

Scientists close in on linchpin of physics, the 'God particle'
Physicists are closing in on a theoretical "God particle" called the Higgs boson that serves as a linchpin in theories of how the universe works at the smallest level.

Hezbollah claims to release CIA names
The exposure creates new security risks for CIA officers in a country where American espionage operations had already been damaged by Hezbollah's capture of a group of agency-paid informants earlier this year.

'Finding Nemo' could get harder
The underwater world in the Disney film is teeming with cheery creatures. But a study says that of the real-life species associated with those in the film, many face the threat of extinction.

Losing one of their own
After a soldier is killed in Afghanistan, the Army's close ties bind his widow and his commander — sometimes uncomfortably.

See More Top Stories

🏠   ◀ ▶   ☰   🔖

Ned's kindle ①   8:58   ⚙ 📶 🔋

Google News   ✕   +

http://news.google.com/   ↻

Web   Images   **News**   Places   more

🔍

Top Stories   Jump to ▾

Hollywood shootout: Music executive dies of injuries
Los Angeles Times - 3 hours ago
A music executive who was critically injured by a gunman who opened fire Friday on
passing motorists in Hollywood has died of the gunshot wounds he sustained, Los
Angeles police said.

msnbc.com

More sources   ⏬

Occupy protesters blocking gates at West Coast ports, halt operations at
some
Washington Post - 16 minutes ago
OAKLAND, Calif. - More than 1000 Occupy Wall Street protesters blocked cargo trucks
at busy West Coast ports Monday, forcing some shipping terminals in Oakland, Calif.

The Guardian

More sources   ⏬

Supreme Court to Rule on Immigration Law in Arizona
New York Times - 2 hours ago
WASHINGTON - In the space of a month, the Supreme Court has thrust itself into the
center of American political life, agreeing to hear three major cases that could help
determine which party controls the House of Representatives and ...

Los Angeles
Times

More sources   ⏬

▌ **World**   Jump to ▾

As Syria Urges Local Voting, UN Puts Toll From Clashes Past 5000
New York Times - 19 minutes ago
BEIRUT, Lebanon - The death toll in the Syrian uprising has exceeded 5000, a United
Nations official said on Monday. Follow @nytimesworld for international breaking news
and headlines.

New York Times

More sources   ⏬

Russian Mogul Joins the Race Against Putin
New York Times - 14 minutes ago
Mikhail D. Prokhorov, who announced his candidacy for the Russian presidency in
Moscow on Monday, passing by a theme restaurant, The American Bar and Grill, after
the news conference.

Globe and Mail

🏠   ◀   ▶   ☰   🔖

Google News - http://news.google.com/

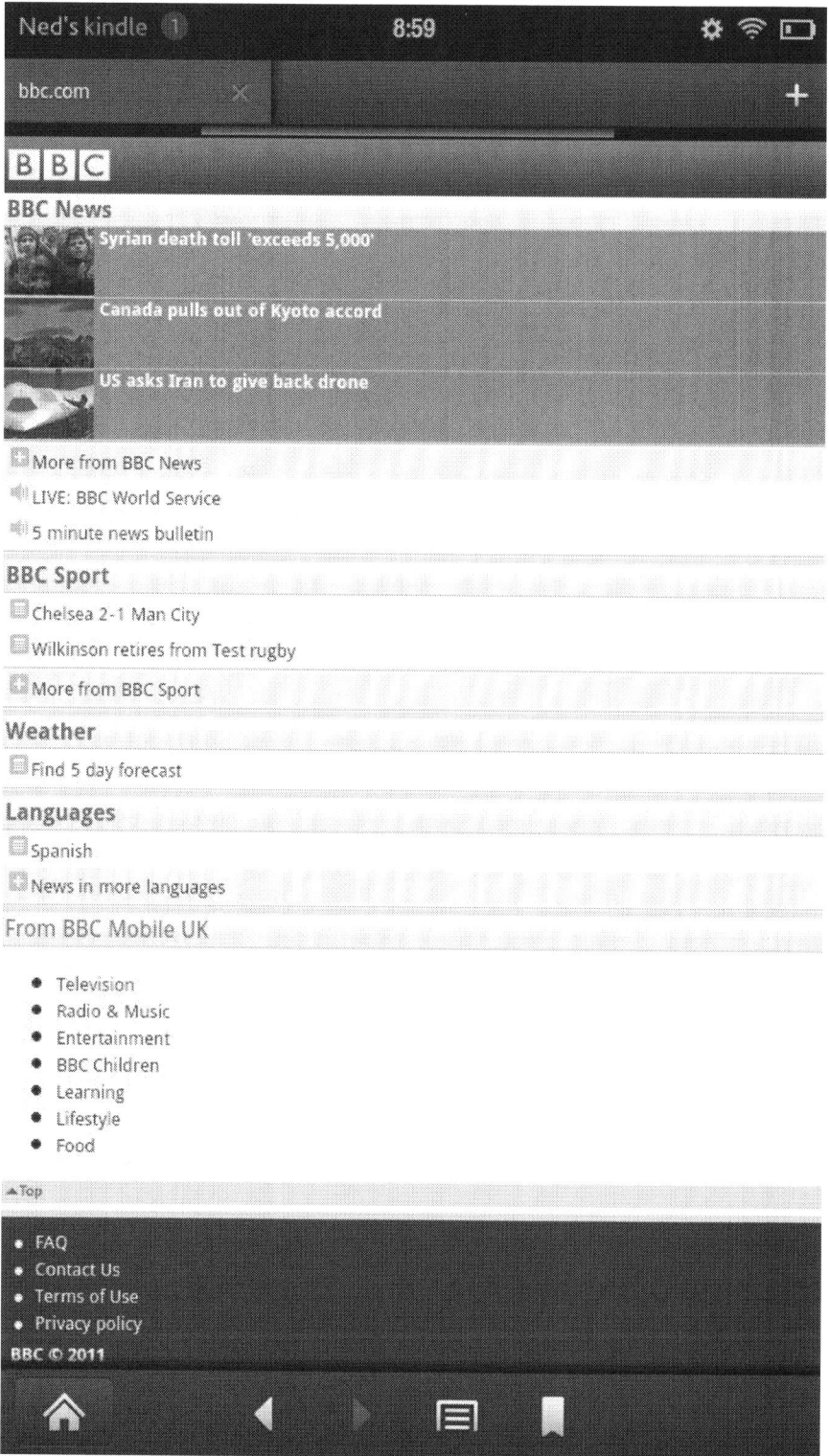

Ned's kindle ① 8:59 ⚙ 📶 🔋

bbc.com ✕ ＋

B B C

BBC News

Syrian death toll 'exceeds 5,000'

Canada pulls out of Kyoto accord

US asks Iran to give back drone

⊞ More from BBC News

◄)) LIVE: BBC World Service

◄)) 5 minute news bulletin

BBC Sport

▢ Chelsea 2-1 Man City

▢ Wilkinson retires from Test rugby

⊞ More from BBC Sport

Weather

▢ Find 5 day forecast

Languages

▢ Spanish

⊞ News in more languages

From BBC Mobile UK

- Television
- Radio & Music
- Entertainment
- BBC Children
- Learning
- Lifestyle
- Food

▲ Top

- FAQ
- Contact Us
- Terms of Use
- Privacy policy

BBC © 2011

🏠 ◄ ▶ ▤ 🔖

BBC - http://www.bbc.co.uk/mobile/i/

Ned's kindle ⓘ   8:59   ⚙ 📶 🔋

Home | m.guardia...   ✕   +

🔲 http://m.guardian.co.uk/   🔄

theguardian
13.12.11
Updated 04.59

Sections   Favourites   Search

Top stories >

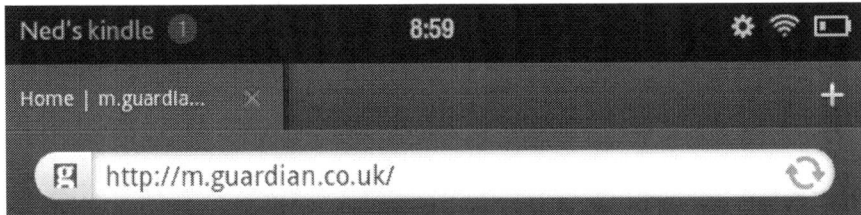

EU summit veto recriminations mount within coalition

Syria: 5,000 dead in violence, says UN human rights chief

Mikhail Prokhorov, Russia's third richest man, to challenge Putin

Sport >

Chelsea 2-1 Manchester City | Premier League match report

Amir Khan battered but belligerent as he demands Peterson rematch

Jonny Wilkinson made all England feel wonderful: we will never forget | Robert Kitson

19:30	Yeovil Town
	Fleetwood Town
19:45	Walsall
	Dagenham and Redbridge
19:45	Oldham Athletic
	Southend United

Latest football scores and fixtures >

Football >

Comment is free >

🏠   ◀   ▶   ☰   🔖

Guardian – http://m.guardian.co.uk

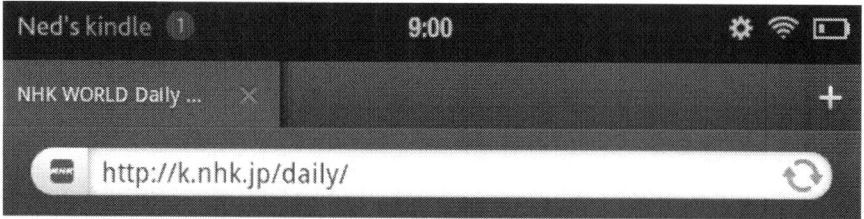

NHK WORLD
Daily News

[HEADLINES]
1. Canada announces withdrawal from Kyoto Protocol
2. Japan's emissions grow in FY2010
3. Lee orders steps against illegal Chinese fishing
4. S.Korea considers guns against illegal fishing
5. Govt decides FY2012 budget compilation outline
6. Over 200 to work at new reconstruction agency
7. Govt maintains export arms ban
8. Fire under control at Tsuruga nuclear plant
9. Areva to post huge loss

0.About This Site

[Other languages]

#.NHK TOP(Japanese)

(c)NHK

Ned's kindle ① 9:01

Reuters|Top News ✕ +

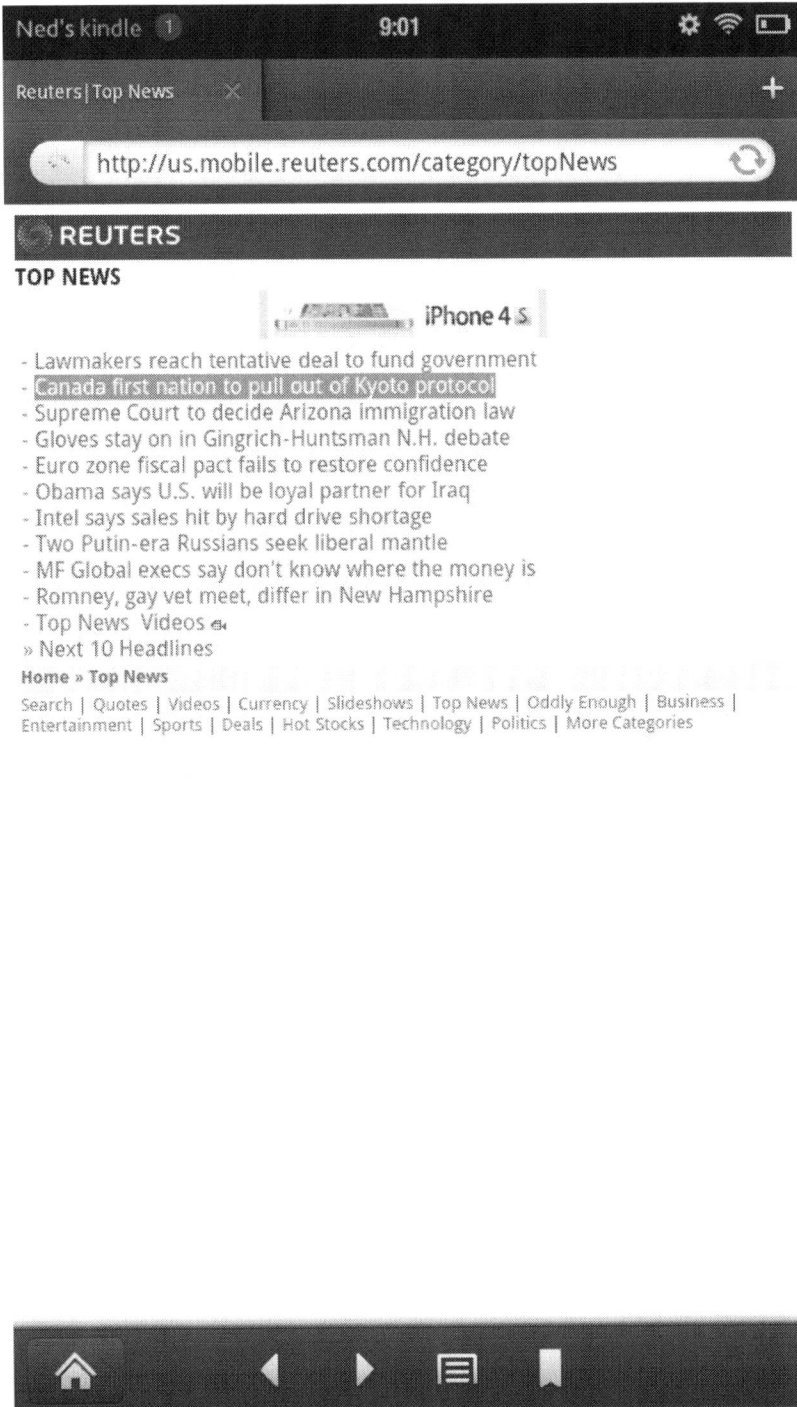

http://us.mobile.reuters.com/category/topNews

REUTERS

TOP NEWS

iPhone 4 S

- Lawmakers reach tentative deal to fund government
- Canada first nation to pull out of Kyoto protocol
- Supreme Court to decide Arizona immigration law
- Gloves stay on in Gingrich-Huntsman N.H. debate
- Euro zone fiscal pact fails to restore confidence
- Obama says U.S. will be loyal partner for Iraq
- Intel says sales hit by hard drive shortage
- Two Putin-era Russians seek liberal mantle
- MF Global execs say don't know where the money is
- Romney, gay vet meet, differ in New Hampshire
- Top News Videos ⬛
» Next 10 Headlines

Home » Top News

Search | Quotes | Videos | Currency | Slideshows | Top News | Oddly Enough | Business | Entertainment | Sports | Deals | Hot Stocks | Technology | Politics | More Categories

Ned's kindle 1   9:02   ⚙ 📶 🔋

The New Yorker ✕   +

🔍 http://www.newyorker.com/   ⟳

THE NEW YORKER

| SUBSCRIBE | IN THE MAGAZINE | BLOGS | AUDIO & VIDEO | LISTINGS |

TABLE OF CONTENTS | HUMOR | NEWS DESK | CULTURE DESK | FICTION | APPS | 2012 ELECTION | WALL ST

2011: THE YEAR IN REVIEW

TEN SIGNS OF A HOT WORLD

BY ELIZABETH KOLBERT

News of a warming planet—how much worse did it get?

KOLBERT: TWO DEGREES OF DISASTER

ALEXIS OKEOWO: TEN UPBEAT AFRICA STORIES

THE YEAR'S BEST SHOUTS & MURMURS

MORE LISTS

‹ • • • • ›

NEWS DESK

TESTING RYAN BRAUN
by Ben McGrath

Plus: Who's holding Robert Levinson?

TO-DO LIST | QUIZ | CRISIS IN A NUTSHELL

CULTURE DESK

AN EVENING WITH JULIAN BARNES
by Lauren Collins

Plus: Santas in the

EDITORS' CHOICE

LETTER FROM EUROPE
THE RISE OF ANGELA MERKEL
by Jane Kramer

From scientist to Chancellor.

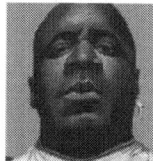

THE SPORTING SCENE
KING OF WALKS
by Ben McGrath

Barry Bonds and the doping scandal.

YEAR IN REVIEW
THE BEST OF 2011

🏠   ◀   ▶   🗐   🔖

New Yorker - http://newyorker.com/

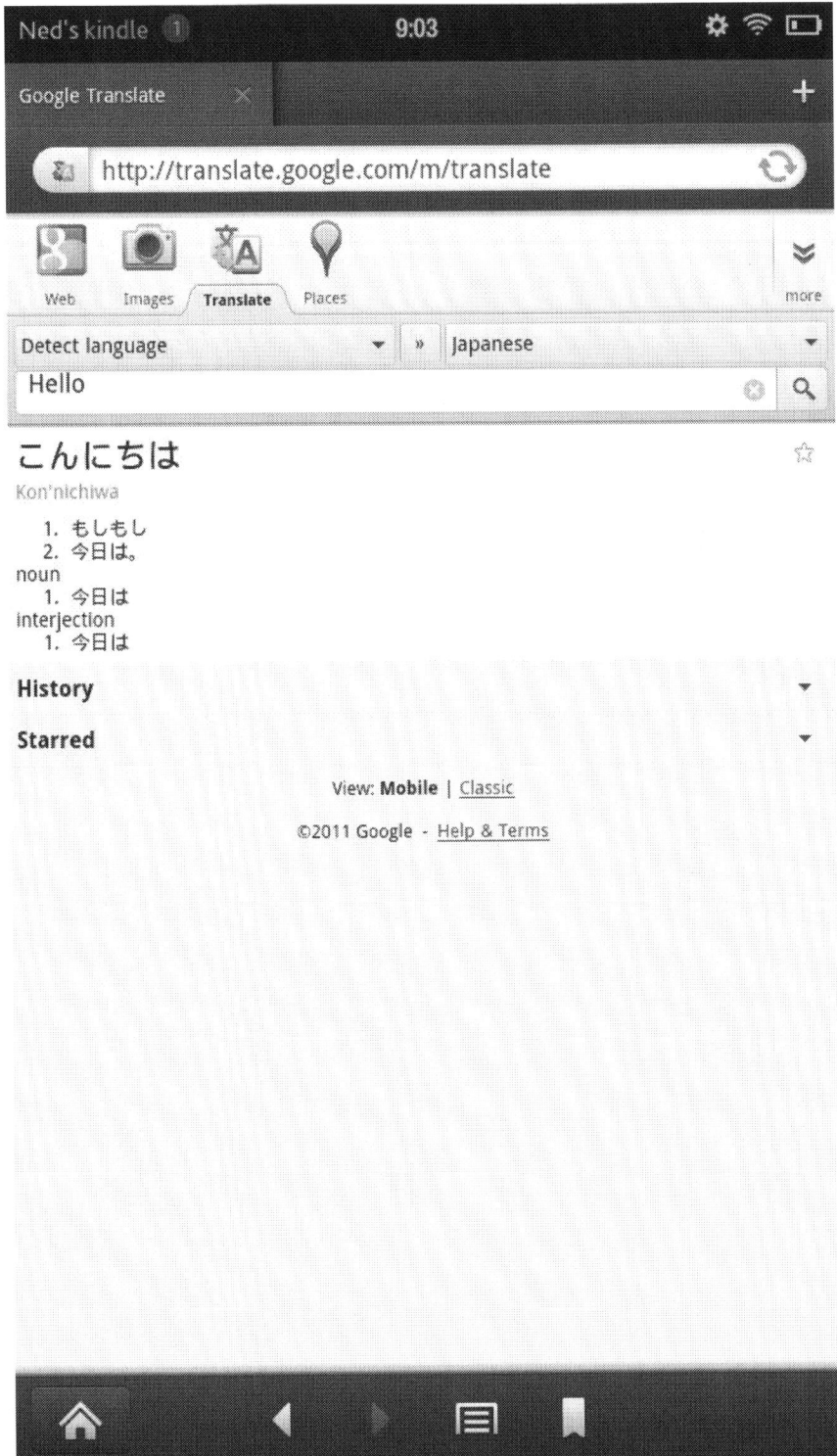

Ned's kindle ① 9:03 ⚙ 🛜 🔋

Google Translate ✕ +

🔖 http://translate.google.com/m/translate ↻

| Web | Images | **Translate** | Places | | more |

Detect language ▼ » Japanese ▼

Hello ⊗ 🔍

こんにちは ☆
Kon'nichiwa

   1. もしもし
   2. 今日は。
noun
   1. 今日は
interjection
   1. 今日は

History ▼

Starred ▼

View: **Mobile** | Classic

©2011 Google - Help & Terms

🏠 ◀ ▶ ☰ 🔖

Google Translate - http://translate.google.com/

Ned's kindle ① 9:13 ⚙ 🛜 🔋

| NAVTEQ TRAFFIC.C... ✕ | + |

http://mobi.traffic.com/traffic/-1-2-1;jsessionid=250E... ↻

NAVTEQ **TRAFFIC.COM**™

New York Area

Zoom In   Zoom Out

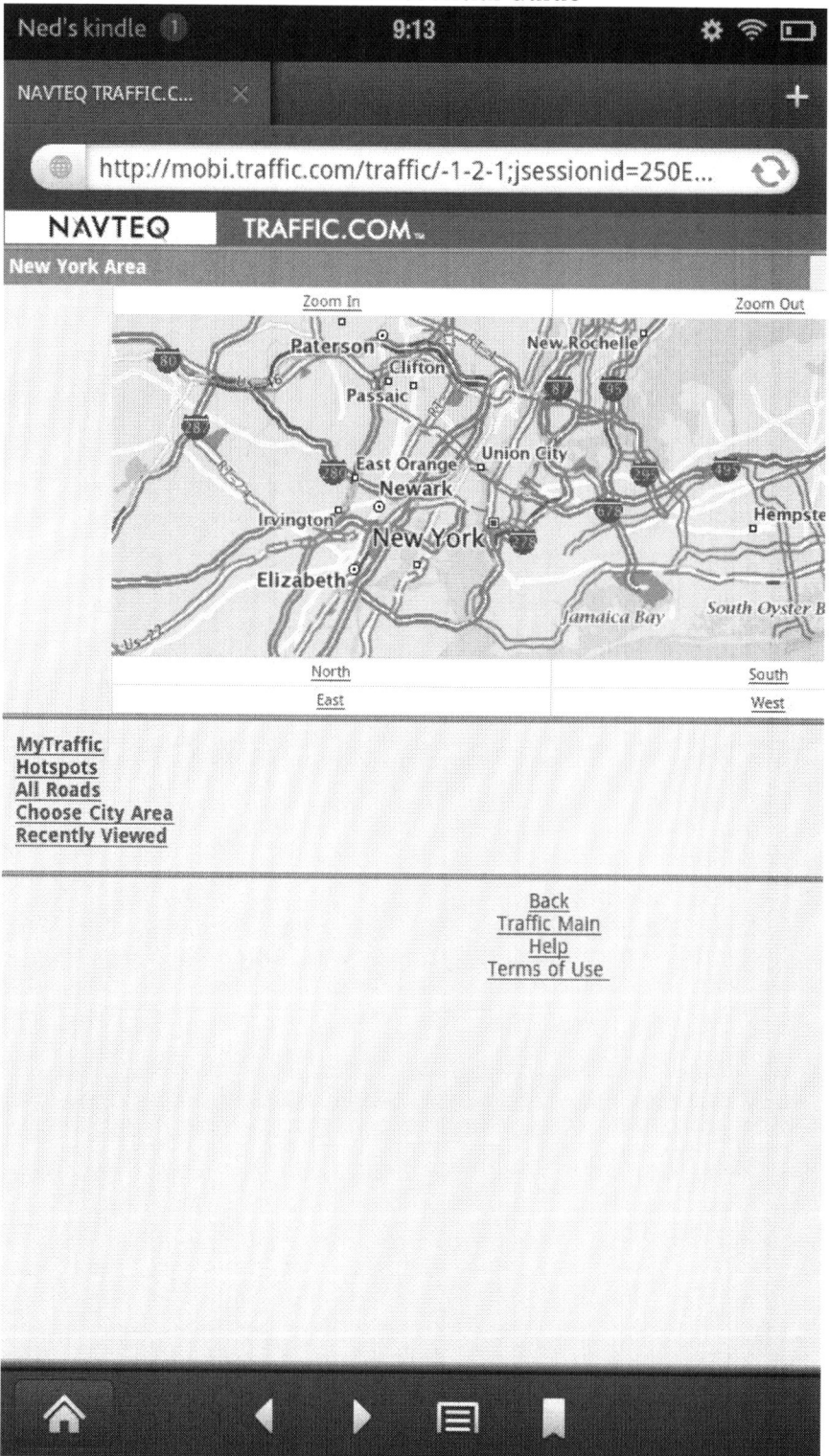

North   South
East   West

MyTraffic
Hotspots
All Roads
Choose City Area
Recently Viewed

Back
Traffic Main
Help
Terms of Use

⌂ ◀ ▶ ☰ ▮

Navteq Traffic.com – http://mobi.traffic.com/

Ned's kindle ①   9:03   ⚙ 🛜 ▭

Wikipedia, the fre...   ✕   +

W   http://en.m.wikipedia.org/?useformat=mobile   ↻

W [   ] 🔍

Today's Featured Article

The **Cogan House Covered Bridge** is a Burr arch truss covered bridge over Larrys Creek in Cogan House Township, Lycoming County, in the U.S. state of Pennsylvania. It was built in 1877 and is 94 feet 2 inches (28.7 m) long. The bridge was placed on the National Register of Historic Places in 1980, and had a major restoration in 1998. The Cogan House bridge is named for the township and village of Cogan House. The covered bridge was constructed by a millwright who assembled the timber framework in a field next to the sawmill, before it was reassembled at the bridge site. It was the only bridge on Larrys Creek that survived the flood of June 1889, and one of only a handful that were left intact in the county. Although the bridge used to carry a steady flow of tannery and sawmill traffic, the clearcutting of the surrounding forests meant the end of those industries by the early 20th century. Since then much of the surrounding area has reverted to second growth forest, and the one-lane bridge is now on a dead end road in a remote valley with little traffic. **(more...)**

Recently featured: Gillingham Football Club – *Californication* – Norwich Market

In The News

- The **United Nations Climate Change Conference** in Durban, South Africa, closes with an agreement to establish a new treaty to limit carbon emissions.
- Allegations of flaws in the Russian legislative elections trigger the country's **largest protests** *(pictured)* since the dissolution of the Soviet Union.
- Iran files a formal complaint to the UN Security Council regarding a U.S. RQ-170 Sentinel aircraft **seized** within its territory.
- The National Basketball Association **lockout** ends with a collective bargaining agreement between players and owners.
- Positive Slovenia, led by Ljubljana mayor Zoran Janković, wins a narrow plurality in the **Slovenian parliamentary election.**

View this page on regular Wikipedia | Disable images on mobile site

Permanently disable mobile site

Text is available under the Creative Commons Attribution-ShareAlike License; additional terms may apply. See Terms of use for details.

🏠   ◀   ▷   ☰   ▮

Wikipedia - http://m.wikipedia.org/

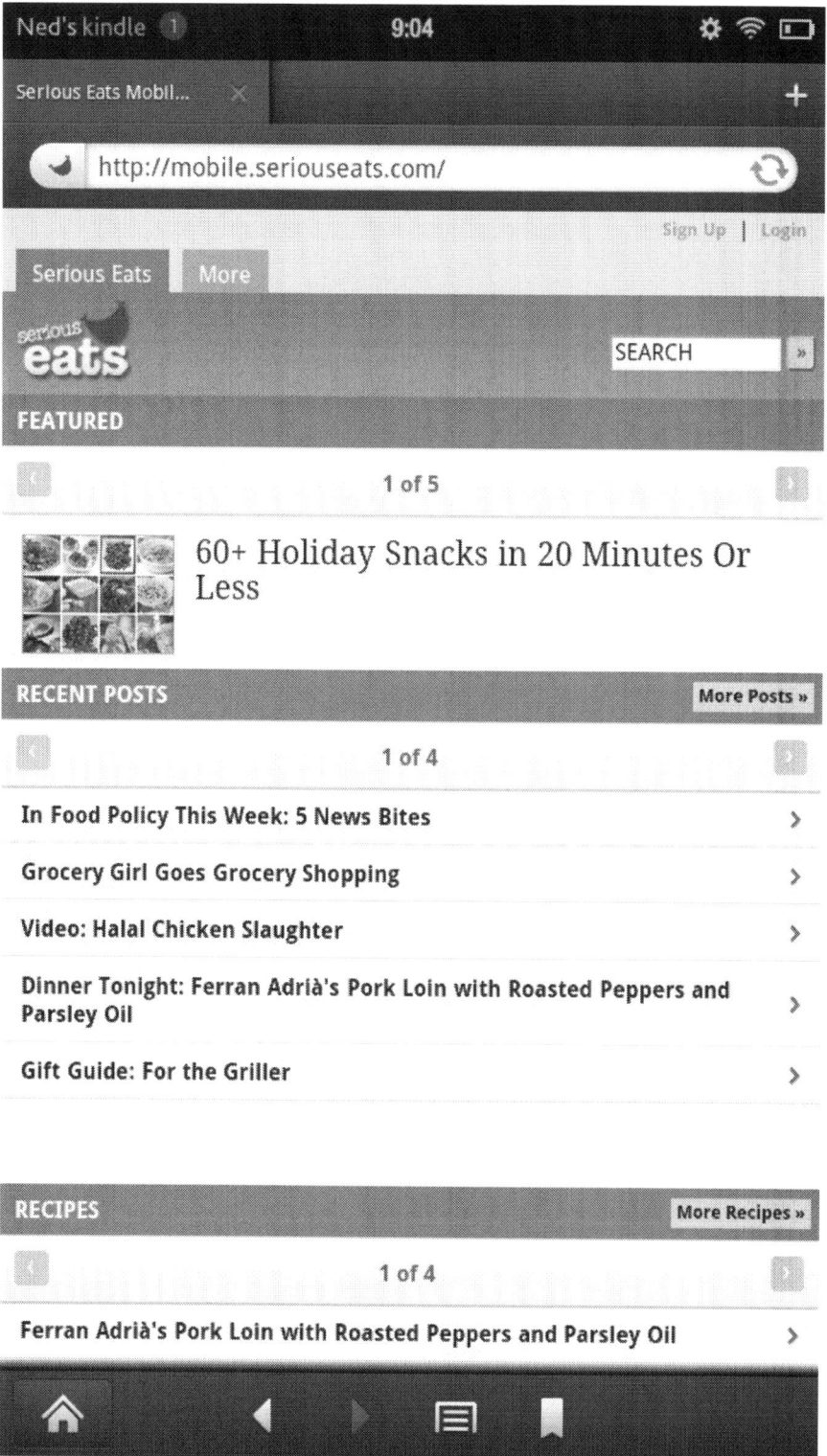

Ned's kindle   1   9:04   ⚙ 🔗 🔋

Serious Eats Mobil...   ✕   +

http://mobile.seriouseats.com/   ↻

Sign Up | Login

Serious Eats   More

serious
eats   SEARCH   »

FEATURED

‹   1 of 5   ›

60+ Holiday Snacks in 20 Minutes Or Less

RECENT POSTS   More Posts »

‹   1 of 4   ›

In Food Policy This Week: 5 News Bites   >

Grocery Girl Goes Grocery Shopping   >

Video: Halal Chicken Slaughter   >

Dinner Tonight: Ferran Adrià's Pork Loin with Roasted Peppers and Parsley Oil   >

Gift Guide: For the Griller   >

RECIPES   More Recipes »

‹   1 of 4   ›

Ferran Adrià's Pork Loin with Roasted Peppers and Parsley Oil   >

🏠   ◀   ▶   ☰   ▮

Ned's kindle 🔘　　　　　　　9:05　　　　　　　⚙ 📶 🔋

MovieTickets ✕ ＋

🎞 http://mobile.movietickets.com/new_releases.asp 🔄

ARTHUR CHRISTMAS　NOW PLAYING
GET TICKETS & SHOWTIMES

m movie tickets.com　　　　　　🅵 Like 93k　MENU

New Releases

12/16/2011

Cook County
(NR) 01:33 »

London River
(NR) 01:27 »

Alvin and the Chipmunks: Chipwrecked
(G) 01:27 »

Sherlock Holmes: A Game of Shadows
(PG-13) 02:08 »

Mission: Impossible - Ghost Protocol: The IMAX
Experience
(PG-13) 02:12 »

Corman's World: Exploits of a Hollywood Rebel
(R) 02:05 »

Young Adult
(R) 01:34 »

Carnage
(R) 01:19 »

🏠　　◀　▶　☰　🔖

MovieTickets.com - http://mobile.movietickets.com/

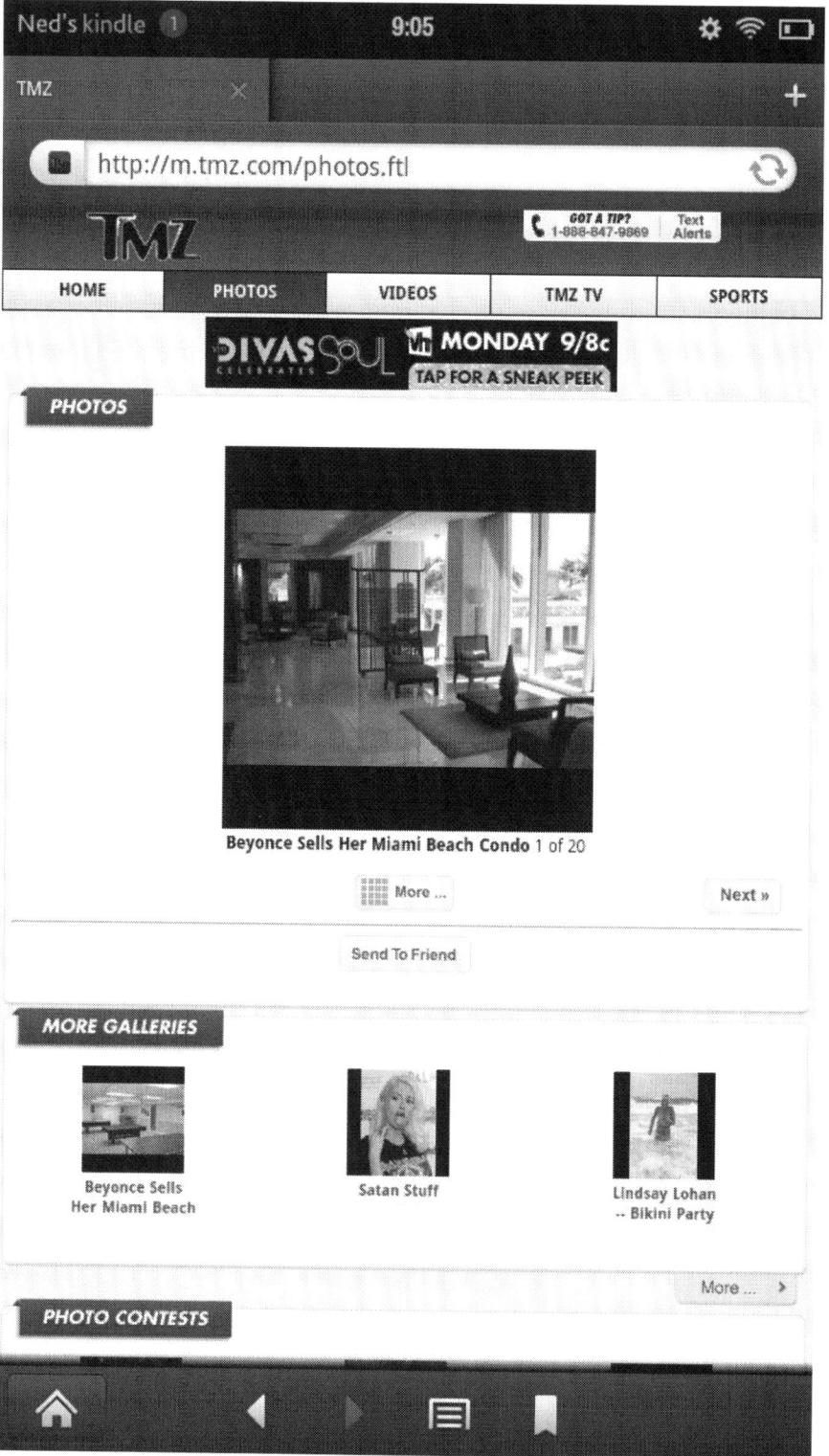

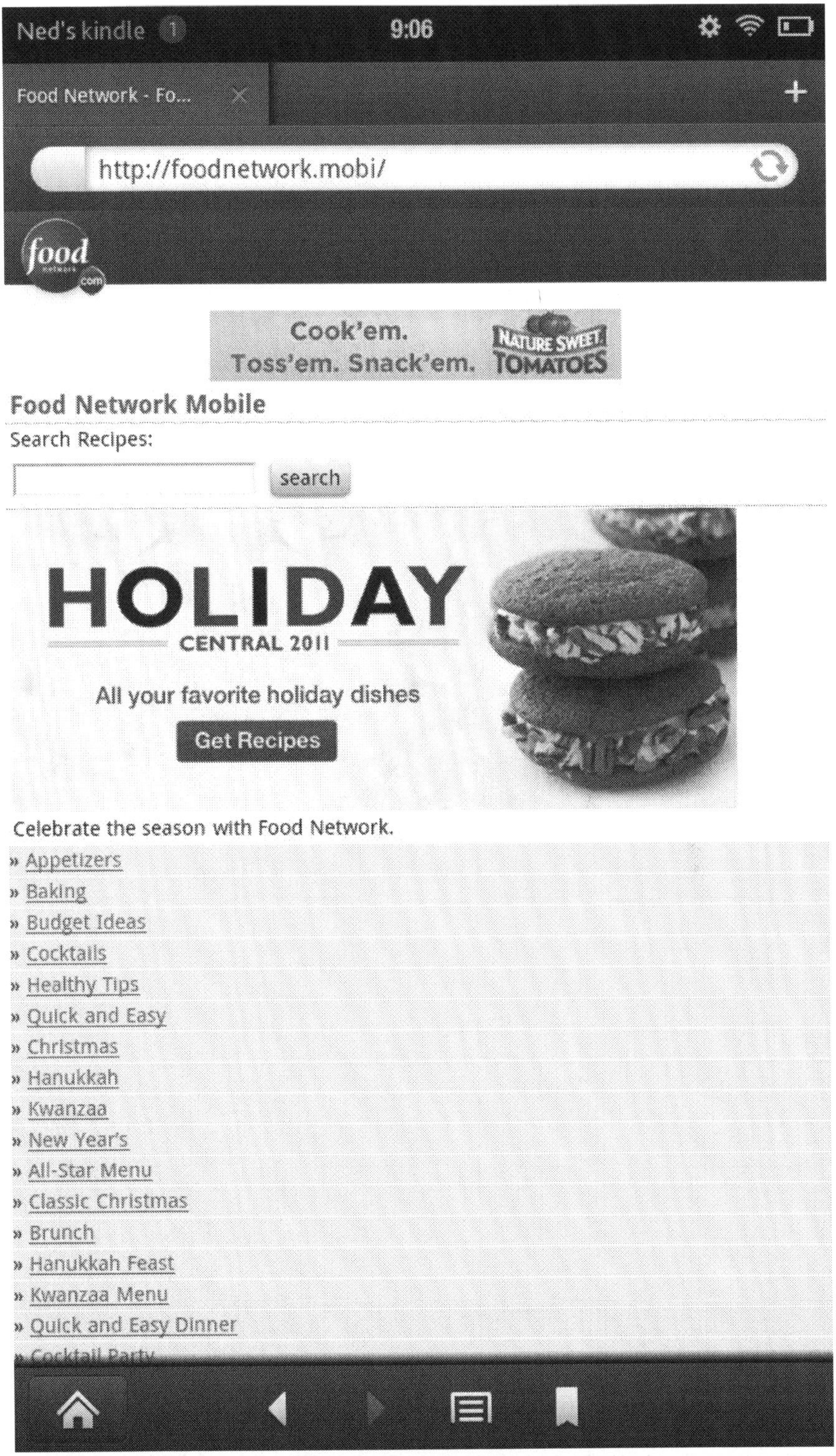

Food Network - http://foodnetwork.mobi/

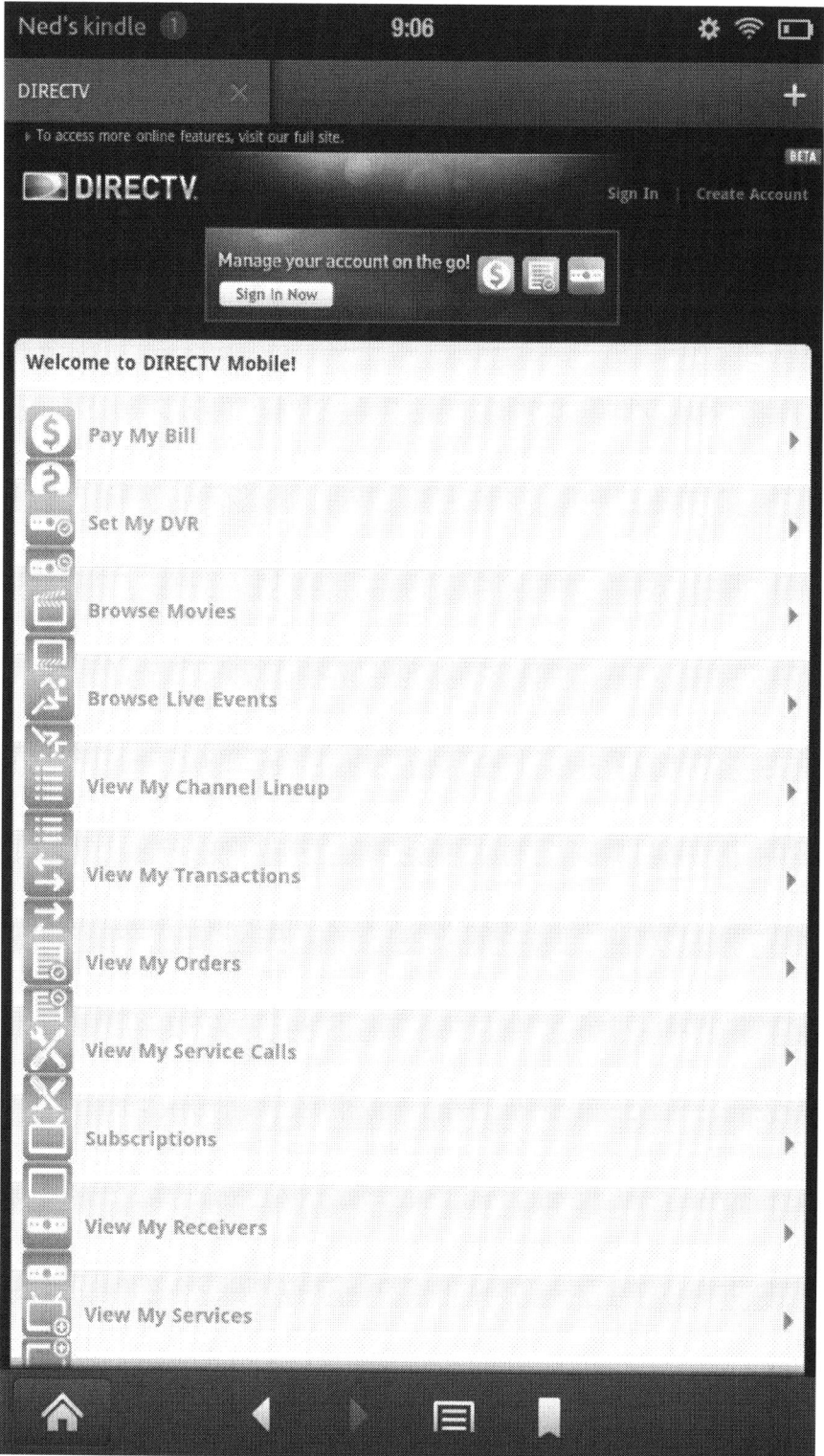

Ned's kindle ①   9:06   ⚙ 🔇 🔋

| DIRECTV | ✕ | ➕ |

▸ To access more online features, visit our full site.

BETA

◼️ DIRECTV.   Sign In | Create Account

Manage your account on the go! $ ▤ ▭
Sign In Now

Welcome to DIRECTV Mobile!

$ Pay My Bill   ▸

? Set My DVR   ▸

▪ Browse Movies   ▸

▪ Browse Live Events   ▸

▪ View My Channel Lineup   ▸

▪ View My Transactions   ▸

▪ View My Orders   ▸

✖ View My Service Calls   ▸

▪ Subscriptions   ▸

▪ View My Receivers   ▸

▪ View My Services   ▸

🏠   ◀   ▶   ▤   🔖

DirecTV Mobile Remote - http://m.directv.com/

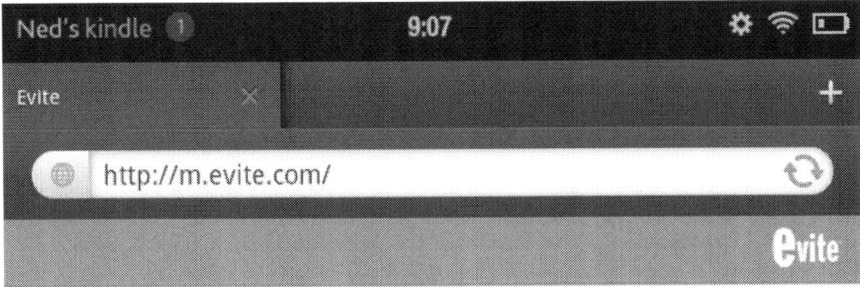

Ned's kindle ① 9:07 ✿ 🛜 ▭

Evite ✕ +

🌐 http://m.evite.com/ ↻

evite

Sign In

Email Address

Password

Sign In

Don't have an Evite Account?

Register Now

Forgot your password?

© 2010 Evite

Terms of Service | Privacy Policy

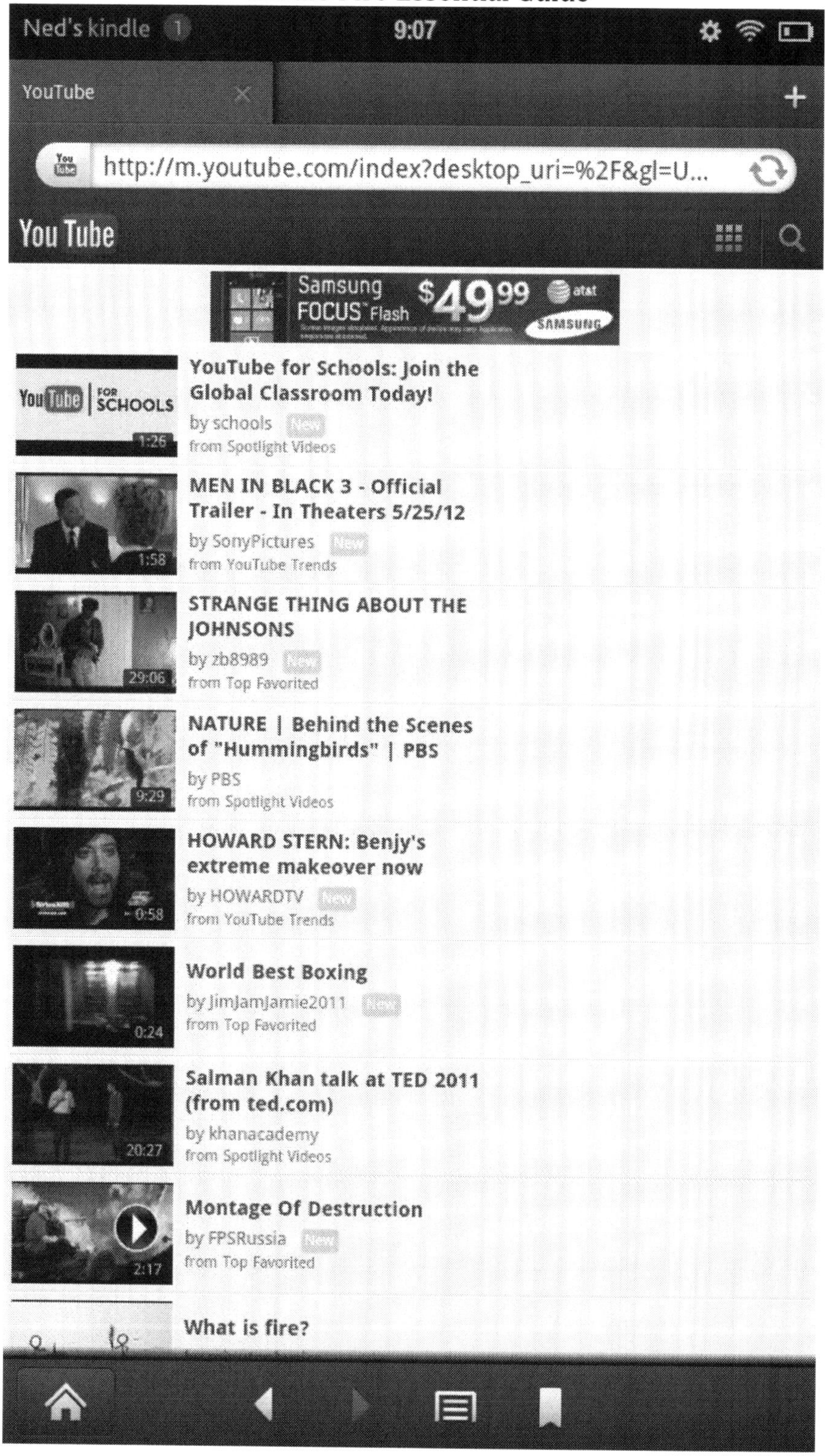

Youtube - http://m.youtube.com/

Ned's kindle ① 9:08 ✱ 🔊 ▭

Flickr ✕ +

http://m.flickr.com/#/explore/interesting/ ↻

flickr from YAHOO! Sign In

| Welcome | **Explore** | Nearby | Search |

Explore / Interesting
12th December, 2011

Page 1 of 21 **Next**

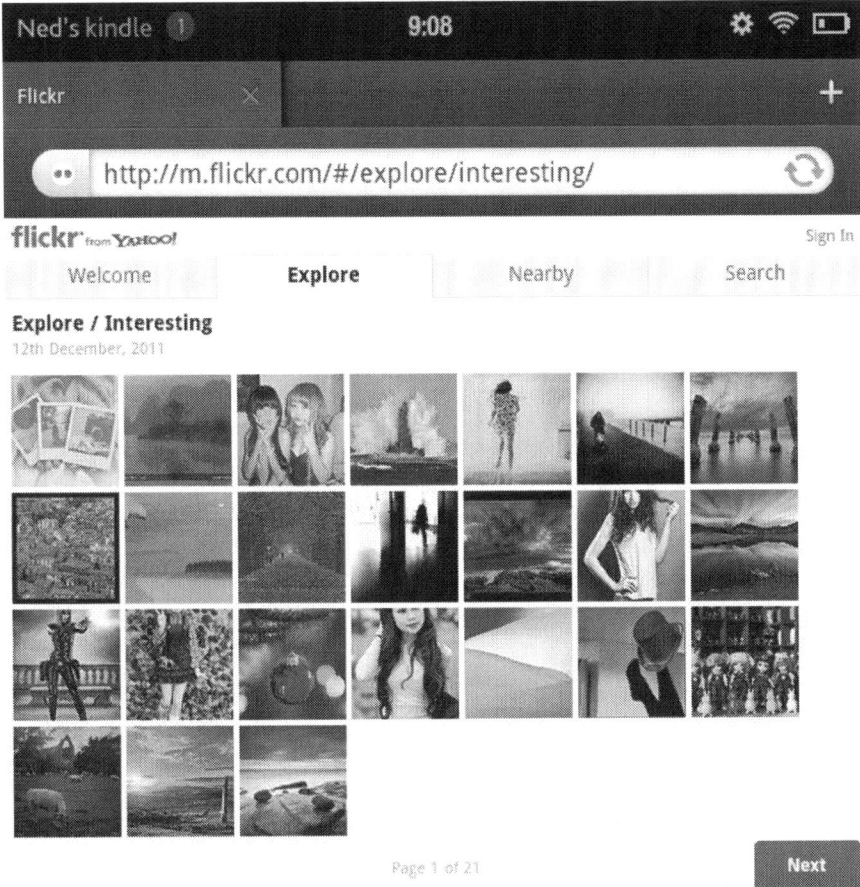

Copyright © 2011 Yahoo! Inc. All rights reserved.
From Yahoo! | Your Privacy | Terms of Use
flickr.com | old m.flickr.com | report abuse

Flickr - http://m.flickr.com/

Ned's kindle 1   9:09   ⚙ 🔊 ▭

PGATour   ✕   +

🌐 http://mobile.pgatour.com/   🔄

PGATOUR.COM   Titleist

| PGA TOUR | CHAMPIONS | NATIONWIDE |

-Menu-   ▼   GO

Hi Guest

Follow your Fav Player, Select Now

PRO V1 AND PRO V1x.
#1 GIFT IN GOLF.

Player Search   🔍

NEWS

Unexpected success continues for Bradley, Steele

Unexpected success continues for Bradley, Steele   ›

Quick 18: Luke's next target, hot Quiros, and skirts   ›

More News ›

Top 5 Players
ephen Gangluff -16 | 3. Bobby Gates -15 | 4. Seung-yul Noh - 15 | 5. Tommy Biershenk -14

LEADERBOARD   SCORING BY

PGA TOUR Qualifying Tournament
Jack Nicklaus Tourn. Course , CA

**Brendon
Todd**
POS 1
SCORE -17

**Stephen
Gangluff**
POS 2
SCORE -16

Full Leaderboard ›

Top 5 Players
Johnson -9 | 3. Paul Casey -5 | 4. Hunter Mahan -4 | 5. Matt Kuchar -4

🏠   ◀   ▶   ☰   🔖

Ned's kindle ① 9:10

NFL.com - The Offi... ✕ +

NFL.COM MENU

CLE	3	IND	10	ATL	31	HOU	20
PIT	14	BAL	24	CAR	23	CIN	19
FINAL		FINAL		FINAL		FINAL	

A 'HAWK OF A PERFORMANCE
The Seahawks played an all-around dominant game en route to a 30-13 thrashing of the Rams.

LATEST NEWS

Dolphins fire Sparano, will seek 'young Don Shula' as coach
The Dolphins fired Tony Sparano, the team announced Monday, and secondary coach Todd Bowles will take over on an interim basis.
Read More

Chiefs fire Haley; GM doesn't see coach as 'mistake'

League, union reps to meet with Browns on McCoy situation

Steelers LB Harrison says hit on McCoy not worth suspension

Elway: Tebow's leadership has changed Broncos' culture

NFL - http://m.nfl.com/

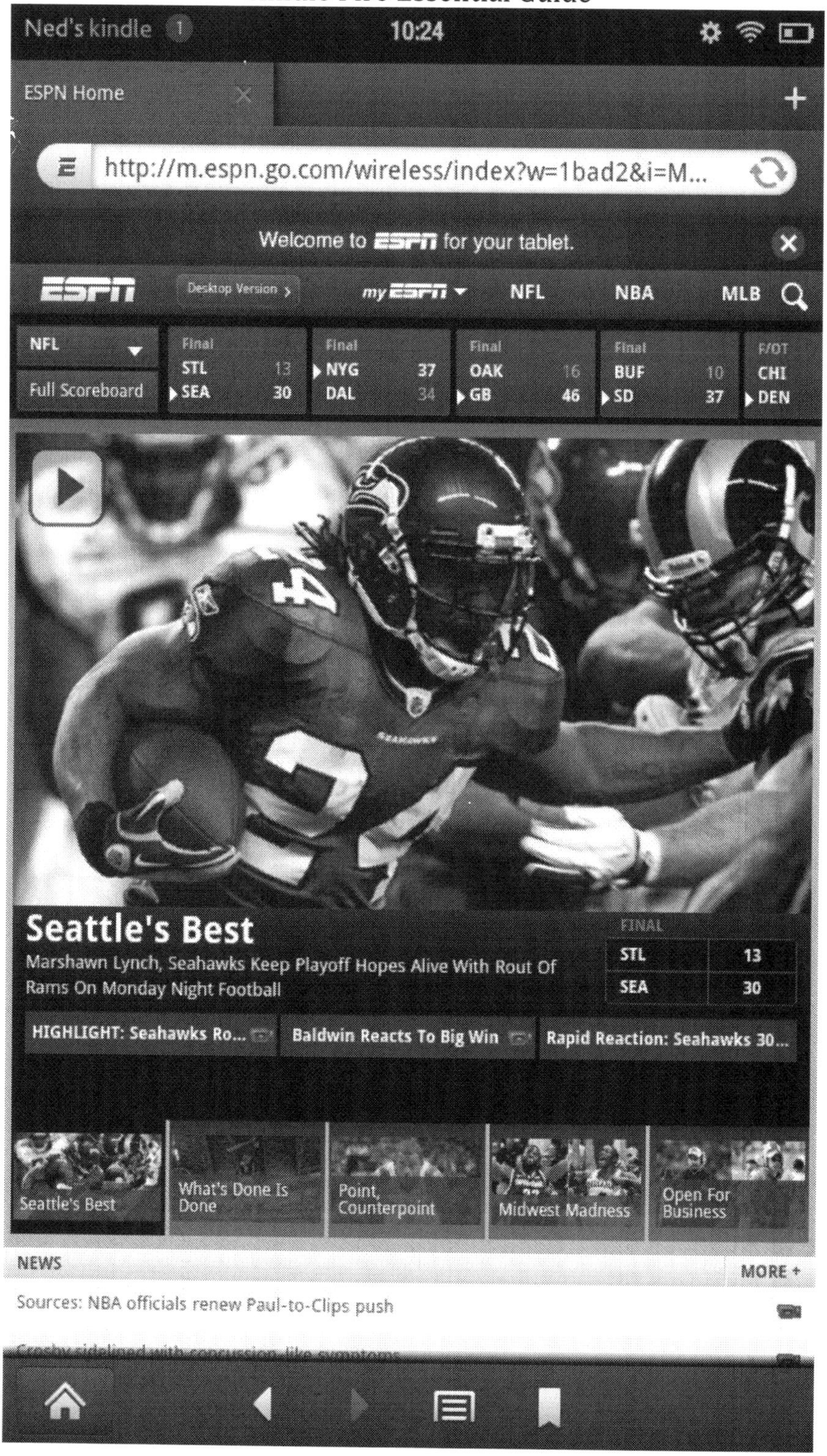

ESPN - http://espn.mobi/

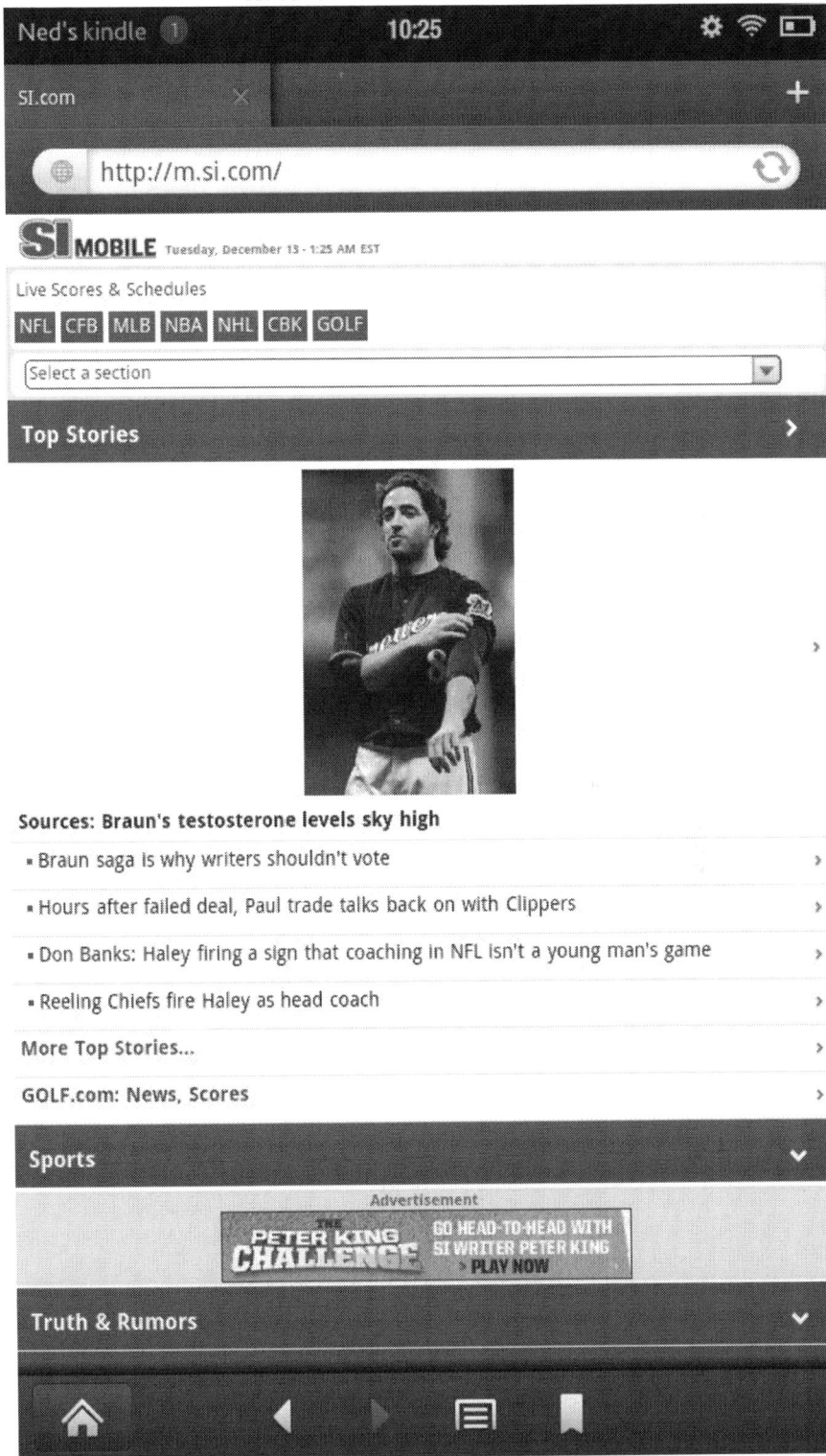

Ned's kindle ①   10:27   ⚙ 🛜 🔋

Soccer News, Resu...   ✕   ＋

○ goal.com mobile   ▤ US ▾   Menu

El totalmente nuevo Nissan VERSA® SEDAN
INNOVACIÓN A TU MEDIDA. INNOVACIÓN PARA TODOS.
CONOCE MÁS   NISSAN

Latest   Scores

Chelsea 2-1 Man City: Unbeaten run ends

Off To Shanghai

U.S. Teammates Square Off

Moyes admits interest in Thierry Henry loan

Tigres 3-1 Santos: Apertura champs

Real Madrid 1-3 Barcelona: Barca to the top

Mourinho: Clasico loss is not a failure

El totalmente nuevo Nissan VERSA® SEDAN
INNOVACIÓN A TU MEDIDA. INNOVACIÓN PARA TODOS.
CONOCE MÁS   NISSAN

Breaking News   Monday, December 12, 2011

7:28 PM -   Marseille president: Valbuena staying put

7:25 PM -   Villas-Boas denies goal celebration story

6:54 PM -   Seattle midfielder Erik Friberg to Malmo FF

6:32 PM -   Edu set for new Rangers contract

6:01 PM -   Mancini: This defeat changes nothing

More Breaking News   ▼

Top News

Teams   ▼

🏠   ◀   ▶   ▤   🔖

Goal.com (Soccer) - http://m.goal.com/

Ned's kindle   10:28

MLB.com Mobile   ✕   +

http://wap.mlb.com/

2011 World Series Champions!
MLB.com shop   SHOP NOW »

MLB.com

| Sections | Teams | Apps | More |

Like   821k   Follow @mlb

TOP HEADLINES

 Aramis headed to Milwaukee, pending physical
Monday, December 12, 2011 9:59 PM ET

 Pirates pick up McGehee in swap with Brewers
Tuesday, December 13, 2011 12:07 AM ET

 Hot Stove MLBlog: News, notes and analysis
Monday, December 12, 2011 10:19 PM ET

VIDEO

 12/12/11: MLB.com FastCast
Tuesday, December 13, 2011 12:06 AM ET

 Blue Jays deal for Francisco
Monday, December 12, 2011 5:14 PM ET

 McGehee traded to Pirates
Tuesday, December 13, 2011 12:24 AM ET

SCOREBOARD

MLB - http://wap.mlb.com/

Ned's kindle ① 10:28 ⚙ 📶 🔋

NHL.com - The Na... ✕ +

http://www.nhl.com/ice/m_home.htm ✕

NHL Menu

JAN 2 1ET

Scores & Schedule ›

MURRAY OUT
The Los Angeles Kings relieved head coach Terry Murray of his duties on Monday, naming assistant coach John Stevens interim head coach.

TOP HEADLINES

Parise, Henrique help Devils edge Bolts 5-4 ›

No time frame for Crosby's return to action ›

Chelios, Suter, Tkachuk enter U.S. Hockey Hall ›

Patrick Kane to star in premiere of 'NHL 36' ›

Latest Headlines ›

Standings ›

Statistics ›

Teams ›

Players ›

Photo Galleries ›

🏠 ◀ ▶ ☰ 🔖

NHL - http://m.nhl.com/

SPRINT CUP SERIES

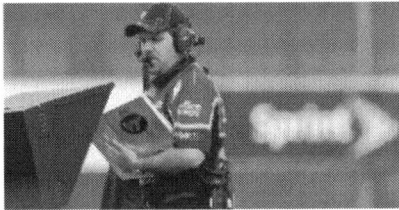

› **Naughty or nice, NASCAR karma comes around**

Just when it seemed it really might not matter who's naughty or nice in NASCAR, two events occurred to restore at least...

TOP STORIES

Breakout performances of 2011: Youth is served

Year in Review: Keselowski positive attitude led to first Chase berth

Preseason staff picks good, but no one predicts champ

Year in Review: Chase mistakes derailed Johnson's drive for sixth title

More

RACE CENTER Ford 400

Official Results

Track: Homestead-Miami Speedway
Time: 03:29:00
Laps: 267

Nascar - http://m.nascar.com/

Ned's kindle 1   10:30   ⚙ 🛜 🔋

Weather Undergro... ✕   +

http://m.wund.com/auto/mobile/?1 🔄

ScanSnap **Paperless life starts here**

wunderground.com

Current   Forecast   Aviation   Models   WunderMap
US Fronts

- Temperature
- Heat Index
- Windchill
- Humidity
- Radar
- Dew Point
- Wind
- Visibility
- Visible Satellite
- Satellite
- Fronts
- Snow Depth
- Precipitation
- Jet Stream
- Flight Rules

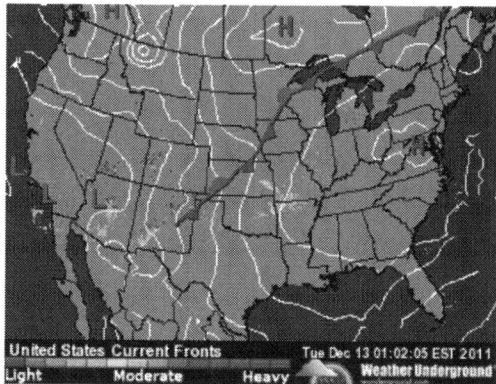

Health Maps

- UV Forecast
- Flu
- Air Quality

United States Current Fronts   Tue Dec 13 01:02:05 EST 2011
Light   Moderate   Heavy   Weather Underground
Updated **6:02 AM GMT on December 13, 2011**

Expand Map   Animate Map

» Set as Default Type
» About These Maps

Pacific - United States - Atlantic   Select a Country or Region

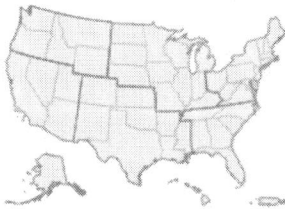

Select a State ▾   Select a Region ▾

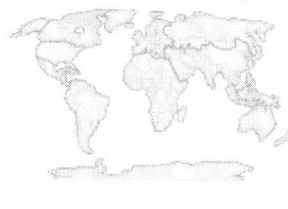

🏠   ◀   ▶   ☰   🔖

Weather Underground - http://m.wund.com/

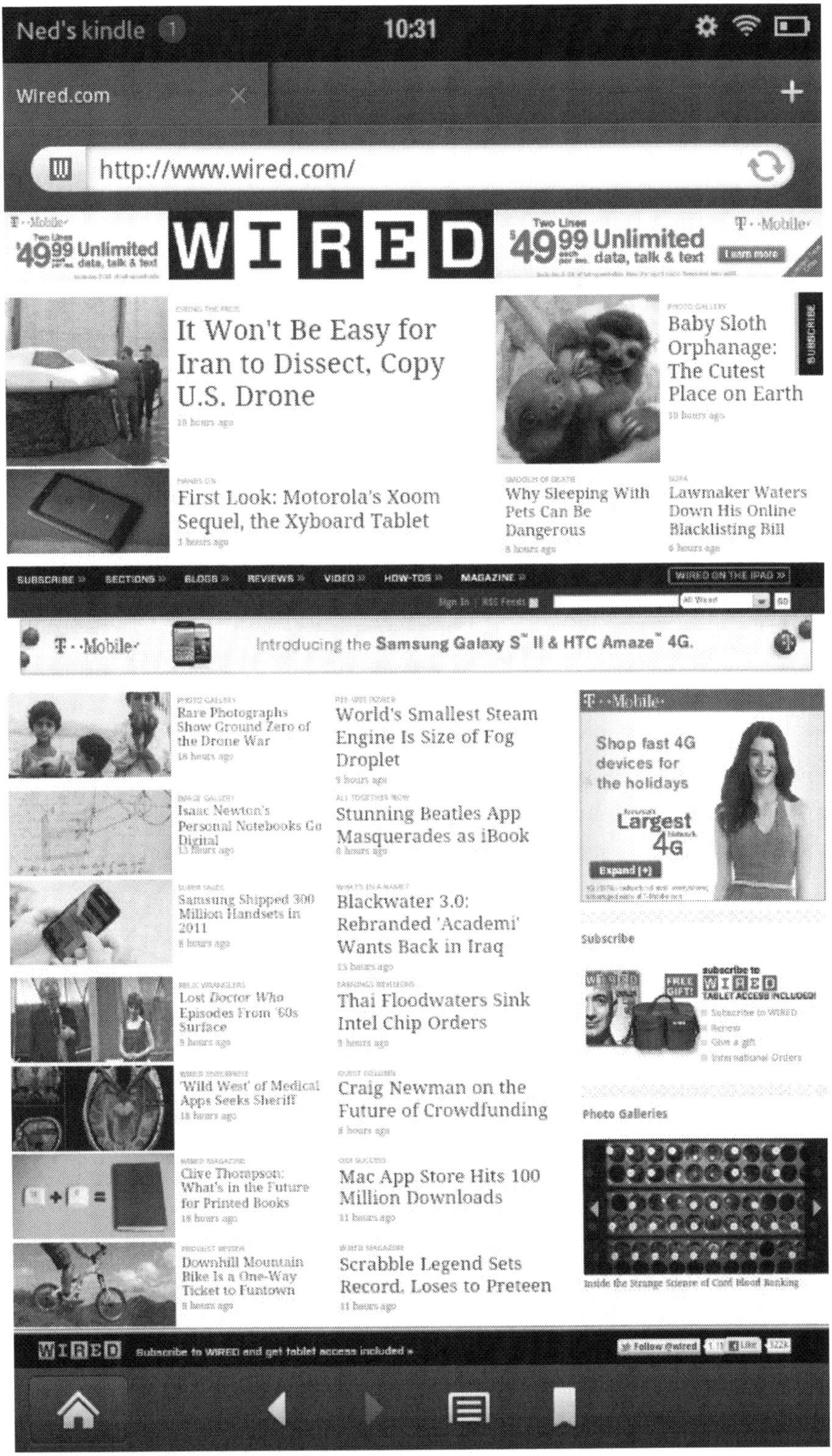

Wired Magazine - http://www.wired.com/

Ned's kindle 1   10:32   ⚙ 📶 🔋

The Huffington Post   ✕   +

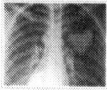

HEALTH-NEWS
ADHD Meds And Your
Heart

CANADA
Clearing The Air In
Attawapiskat?

HIGH-SCHOOL
Star Style: Young Celebs
With Fashion Lines!

CRIME
Missing Mom's Body
Found 2 Miles From Tenn.
Home

WEIRD-NEWS
Infamous Strip Club To Be
Turned Into Church

TECHNOLOGY
BLACKOUT?

LOS-ANGELES
The Biggest Flakes In The
State

STYLE
DOPPELGANGER

SAN-FRANCISCO
THE MEAN STREETS

POLITICS
'PERSONAL FIDELITY'

RELIGION
Philip Clayton, Ph.D.:
Science, Religion And

Huffington Post - http://www.huffingtonpost.com/blackberry/

Ned's kindle ①   10:33   ⚙ 🛜 🔋

http://mobile.theo...   ✕   ＋

Watch The Onion On TV- Fridays at 10p/9c - Only On IFC

⌀ the ONION

Latest   Videos   Images   Sports   Search

The Week In Pictures
SLIDESHOW 12.12.11

+ Share

Drug Addict Looking For More Enabling Girlfriend
RADIO NEWS 12.12.11

+ Share

2011's Most Influential People In Economic News
SLIDESHOW 12.12.11

+ Share

Change of Command
EDITORIAL CARTOON 12.12.11

+ Share

Pop Star's Single, 'Booty Wave', Most Likely Civilization's Downfall
VIDEO 12.12.11

+ Share

Download K'Ronikka's Single 'Booty Wave' Now
BLOG 12.12.11

+ Share

2011: The Economy
AMERICAN VOICES 12.12.11

+ Share

🏠   ◀   ▶   ☰   🔖

The Onion - http://mobile.theonion.com/

Many others exist.

Have fun exploring and discovering new web sites! The iPhone or Mobile version of a website is what you should look for when navigating the web. The Kindle Fire is still a new device so it may take some time for web and content developers to create and target content to all Kindle Fire users.

Kindle Fire Friendly Push / IMAP E-Mail Providers

The following email providers have been confirmed working with the Amazon Fire:

Yahoo! Mail
http://mail.yahoo.com/

Aol
http://mail.aol.com

Fastmail
http://fastmail.fm/

Hotmail
http://hotmail.com/

MobileMe
http://icloud.com/

Gmail
http://gmail.com/

Lavabit
http://lavabit.com/

Adding apps to the Amazon Marketplace

If you are a developer and are looking to add your Android Application to the Store it's easier than you think. For more information visit http://developer.amazon.com/ and click Amazon Appstore for Android.

If you are not a developer and are still interested in creating an application don't be discouraged. If you post your app idea to a freelancer site such as **freelancer.com** or something similar you have the ability to set pricing and have software engineers bid for you to pick them to build your app. Pricing varies so be sure to get a quote before you choose anyone specific. Always use milestone payments and never, ever, release a payment before the job is completed. Freelance is the way to go if you do not want to take the time to learn the skills necessary to build apps yourself.

You can also ask developers of Apps that exist on the Marketplace to add their app to the Amazon Store by contacting them via their website. Sometimes it doesn't take much work so this is an attractive option if you are migrating from one Android device to the Kindle Fire.

Amazon Appstore for Android

Market your apps to tens of millions of customers using Amazon's proven capabilities. Submit your app once for the potential to reach customers on Kindle Fire, the Amazon Appstore mobile client, and online. Learn more about compatibility in our Kindle Fire FAQs.

(from http://developer.amazon.com)

Kindle Fire Technical Information

The Kindle Fire User-Agent String is:

Mozilla/5.0 (Linux; U; Android 2.3.4; en-us; Kindle Fire Build/GINGERBREAD) AppleWebKit/533.1 (KHTML, like Gecko) Version/4.0 Mobile Safari/533.1

or

Mozilla/5.0 (Macintosh; U; Intel Mac OS X 10_6_3; en-us; Silk/1.1.0-80) AppleWebKit/533.16 (KHTML, like Gecko) Version/5.0 Safari/533.16 Silk-Accelerated=true

The Kindle Fire User-Agent String with Privacy Enabled:

Mozilla/5.0 (Macintosh; U; Intel Mac OS X 10_6_3; en-us; Silk/1.1.0-80) AppleWebKit/533.16 (KHTML, like Gecko) Version/5.0 Safari/533.16 Silk-Accelerated=false

This could be useful when looking at your server logs or if you need to easily redirect Kindle Fire users to a specific page using Javascript or PHP.

Screen Resolution

The Kindle Fire has a screen resolution 1024 x 600. Older monochrome Kindle devices have a resolution of 600 x 800.

Display Information

The Kindle Fire has a 1024x600 diagonal display capable of 16 million colors.

Wireless Adapter Information

Wireless comes standard on the Kindle Fire, featuring 802.11b/g/n WiFi.

Targeting Kindle Fire users on the Web

Because the Kindle Fire is fairly new many sites do not fully support or target the exact dimension of the Kindle Fire screen.

Using the follow meta viewport tag will allow Kindle Fire users to view your content at a scale that is perfect for the Kindle Fire screen as well as other mobile devices.

```
<meta name="viewport" content="initial-scale=1.0, width=device-width,
height=device-height, minimum-scale=1.0, maximum-scale=1.0, user-
scalable=no" />
```

If the content on your page does not display well on the Kindle fire using the meta viewport tag redirect Kindle Fire users to a page or section of your site specific to them by using Javascript:

```
<script language="javascript">
<!--
if((navigator.userAgent.match(/Silk-Accelerated/i)) ||
(navigator.userAgent.match(/Kindle Fire/i)))
{
location.href='http://www.mydomain.com/kindlefire/';
}
-->
</script>
```

How to take a Screenshot on the Kindle Fire

Taking a screenshot is an advanced topic and because o
this it is listed here in the very back of the book. Use the
instructions that follow to take a screenshot of your Kindle
Fire screen.

Requirements:

- Kindle Fire
- 2.0 A Male to Micro B USB Cable
- Mac or PC
- TextWrangler file editing software

(The instructions here are for the Mac but would be
similar on the PC.)

To begin download the latest Android SDK from

http://developer.android.com/sdk/index.html

The Android SDK is available for the Mac, Linux and
Windows OS.

Download and unzip the files to a folder on your Desktop
or somewhere you are comfortable with and can
remember.

Open Terminal on the Mac. Use spotlight and type Term
to quickly find this if needed.

Type the following. Type enter after each line:

cd /
cd users
cd Desktop
cd yourfolder (replace with your folder)

cd android-sdk-mac_x86
cd tools

Launch the Android SDK manager with the following command:

./android

The Android SDK Manager should now be loaded on your screen:

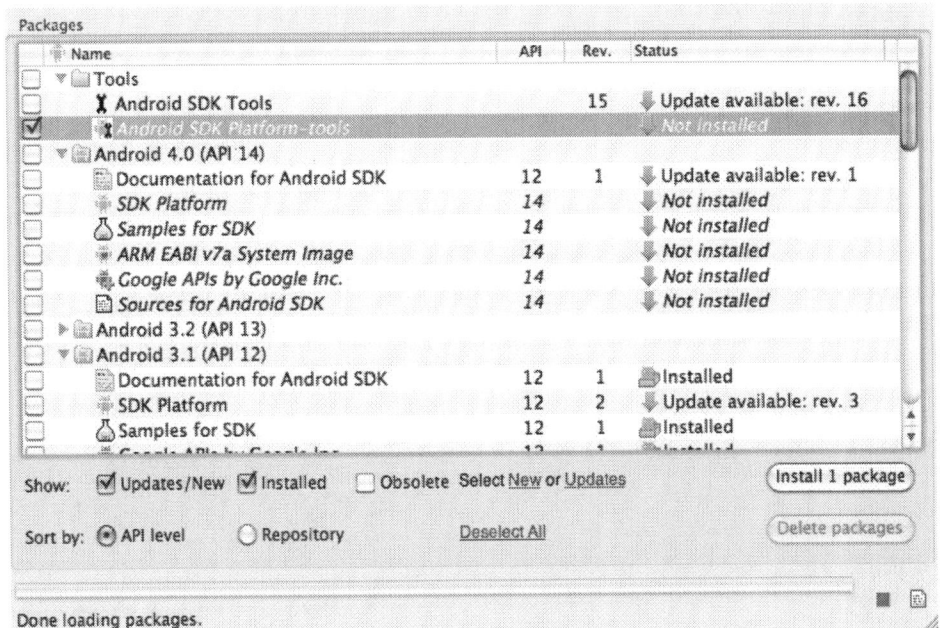

Unselect everything except for Android SDK Platform-tools as shown above. Then click Install 1 package.

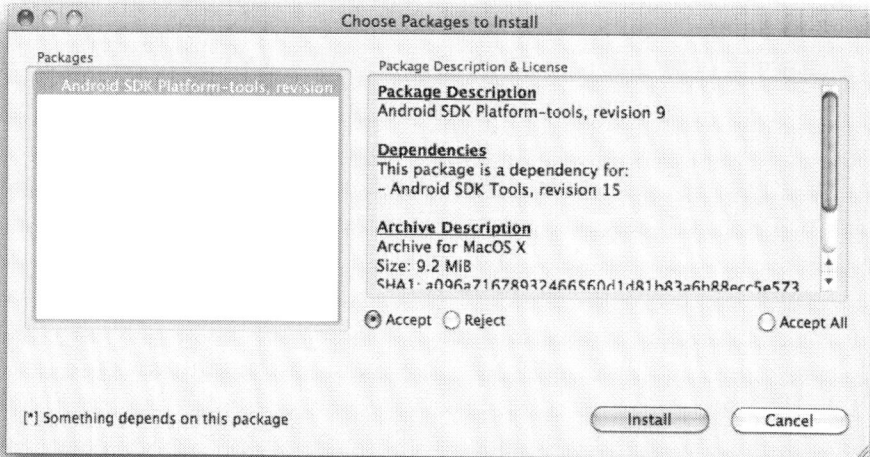

Ensure Accept is selected then choose Install.

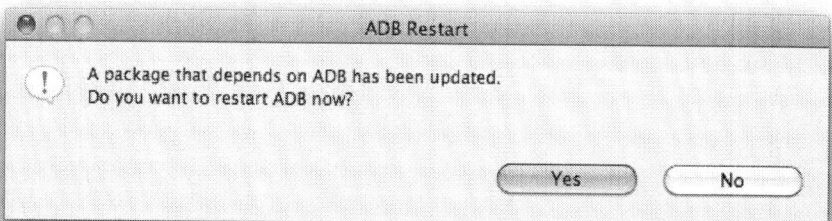

Choose yes when asked to restart ADB.

When you see "Done loading packages." click Done.

Close the Android SDK Manager.

Return to terminal.app

Type **cd ../platformtools**

Type **./adb devices**

Now we need to edit a specific file named adb_usb.ini to do this open a new terminal window. Now type cd .android exactly how it appears.

cd .android

touch adb_usb.ini

open –a TextWrangler adb_usb.ini

TextWrangler will now open.

Place your cursor on the line below the last line. Then type the following:

0x1949

Choose File – Save As – Line Breaks Unix – Encoding UTF-8

Return to the terminal window and type:

cat adb_usb.ini

Close this terminal window.

Return to the previous terminal window.

Type **./adb kill-server** (to stop the server)

Type: **./adb start-server**

"daemon started successfully" will be displayed.

Now. Plug in your Kindle Fire to the USB cable connected to your computer. You will see the following screen display on your Kindle Fire:

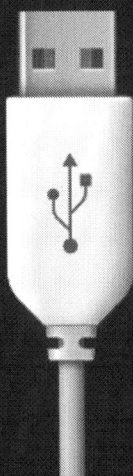

You can now transfer files from your computer to Kindle.

When you are done, press the disconnect button at the bottom of the screen or eject your Kindle from your computer, and then disconnect the USB cable.

On your Kindle Fire press the grey disconnect button.

Return to your computer and type the following:

./adb devices

cd ../tools

./ddms to open the Dalvik Debug Monitor

Select com.amazon.kindle (your device).

> wsj.reader_t3:remote
> com.pandora.android
> wsj.reader_t3
> com.amazon.kindle

Now this is where the magic happens.

On your keyboard press **Command S**.

Device Screen Capture will appear.

Press **rotate** until the image is aligned how you would like.

Press **save** to save the image.

Be sure to add .png to the end of the filename. This is not done for you automatically.

Well, that was easy wasn't it? **Congratulations on taking your first screenshot with the Kindle Fire.**

The process is almost identical for windows users with the exception that the folder structure may be different than the examples listed above.

Kindle Owners' Lending Library Download

If you would like to download the electronic version of this book to review for free from the Kindle Owners' Lending Library follow these instructions:

From your device main screen select Books.

Tap Store in the top-right corner to open the Store.

On the right-hand side tap:

"Kindle Owners' Lending Library".

Tap Computers & Internet.

Now type "Kindle Fire Essential Guide" in the search box at the top of the screen. Select it when it appears on the screen with the price $0.00 with the Amazon Prime logo.

Tap "Borrow for Free" to download the electronic version of this book to your device.

This is a great way for you to discover how to download titles from the Lending Library. Not all publishers and authors include their content on the Kindle Owners Lending Library because it requires exclusivity of the electronic format of the book. The library is growing so be sure to check it often to check out your favorite books for free.

Note that an Amazon Prime membership is required for you to use the Kindle Owners' Lending Library for free. Each title that you borrow from the Library is yours for as long as you like. However, you may only borrow one title each month so keep this in mind when you are choosing the next great book.

For more information about Amazon Prime visit:

http://www.amazon.com/prime/

Notes

Notes

Printed in Great Britain
by Amazon.co.uk, Ltd.,
Marston Gate.

2613316R00073